YOU DON'T NEED LUCK

You Don't Need Luck

Empowering Parents and Inspiring Kids

YOUNGCHAN ANDREW TO

To Future Media LLC

This book is dedicated to my three beautiful children: Lauren To, Andrew To, and Kristen To. Also, I dedicate this book to my wonderful wife, Regina To, who has stood by my side and whom I love and cherish.

Contents

Editor's Preface

July 20th, 2023. I'm a bit unsure about why my preface would come before the author's in this book, but because of his resolute insistence, I've carefully arranged things as he asked. I don't have a lot of words to share, but what I want to tell you is that this book is truly wonderful. It's full of stories that can make you feel different things – some are touching, some are funny, and some are sad. And when it's all said and done, isn't that just how life is?

But the words that truly come from my heart are that I feel incredibly honored and proud to be the one editing this book. Dad, you've been there for me through good times and tough times. And as we continue through all the ups and downs, I want to be right there beside you, supporting and walking with you, now and in the future.

With love,
Lauren To

Author's Preface

June 29, 2023. When I first heard the news of the Supreme Court striking down affirmative action in college admissions, I was filled with a mix of emotions. Anger, frustration, and disappointment all welled up inside me. As a parent, it hit close to home, as I couldn't help but think about my own child's unsuccessful attempts to gain admission into a better college. It felt like a dollar too short and a day too late.

However, amidst this storm of emotions, I realized that my anger could be a powerful catalyst for change. It served as a wake-up call, propelling me to take action and channel my thoughts and frustrations into something meaningful. And so, the idea for this book was born.

In addition to exploring broader societal values and principles, this book will also weave in my personal narratives and real-life events by sharing my own experiences as a parent, husband, and son. Through these personal anecdotes, I can humanize the larger conversation and shed light on the emotional toll, challenges, and frustrations that individuals and families face when navigating the college admissions process in a changing landscape. By intertwining these personal stories with the larger societal discussion, the book can offer a more holistic and comprehensive understanding of the topic.

While my initial anger may have fueled the creation of this work, I recognize that anger alone is not enough. It must be coupled with understanding, empathy, and a commitment to positive change. Therefore, as you read through these pages, I encourage you to approach the topics with an open mind, ready to challenge your own beliefs and consider alternative perspectives.

It is my sincere hope that this book will contribute to a more nuanced and informed discourse on life, and the pursuit of better education. May it inspire readers to question the status quo, engage in meaningful dialogue, and work towards a more equitable future for all.

With determination and a firm belief in the power of words to effect change,

Andrew To

Chapter 1

Introduction

In this book, I humbly share my personal journey as a parent, husband, and son. I wish I could claim that I always got everything right, but the truth is that I am far from perfect. I've faced numerous challenges and encountered seemingly insurmountable obstacles along the way.

I offer my story not as a testament to perfection but as a testament to the human spirit's resilience and capacity for growth. In sharing both my triumphs and shortcomings, I hope to provide a realistic portrayal of the multifaceted nature of these roles.

While there are undoubtedly countless individuals who have excelled in the realms of parenthood, marriage, and filial duty, I firmly believe that each person's journey is unique and valuable. By offering my personal anecdotes and insights, I aim to connect with readers on a personal level and create a space for self-reflection and growth.

As you immerse yourself in the stories within this book, my sincere hope is that you will find enjoyment, laughter, and perhaps even tears. Beyond the entertainment value, I aspire for these tales to resonate deeply with you, provoking introspection and encouraging a fresh perspective on your own path as a parent, child, or spouse.

Thank you for joining me on this heartfelt exploration, and I hope that my experiences resonate with you and provide guidance on your own path.

~

For the longest time, I have harbored a desire to become a writer. I always have an abundance of ideas, but I have been too lazy to embark on any new endeavors. Writing a substantial book requires an immense amount of time and effort, which led me to give up before even attempting to write my own story.

Yet, here I am now, in the process of writing something that may one day be read and used by someone, with the hope that it can bring about a positive change in their life.

My intelligent daughter, Lauren, often asks me, "How smart am I, Daddy?" I always respond by saying that she is average, emphasizing that she needs to work harder than others to succeed.

Lauren is undeniably a brilliant child, and it's not just because she shares my blood. Her recent IQ test scored over 140, she skipped a grade (could have skipped more if we wanted to), published a book at the age of 14, initiated a nonprofit free tutoring program that operates district-wide around the same age, and maintains the top position in her class. However, I hesitate to acknowledge her intelligence openly because I genuinely fear that it might foster laziness within her. History has shown that a highly intelligent individual with a lazy attitude often ends up in unfavorable circumstances. Thus, I would prefer to have a child with an average intellect but a diligent work ethic.

Lauren has a voracious appetite for reading and constantly seeks out bigger and more challenging material. When I began teaching her multiplication tables, she quickly expressed her desire to learn two-digit multiplication, three-digit multiplication, and beyond. Our trips to the local used bookstore became a bit overwhelming, as she devoured the $2 chapter books faster than I could keep up. To satisfy her insatiable thirst for knowledge, we turned to the local public library, where we would check out 10-15 books every week.

Personally, I hadn't visited a library in ages, except for the occasional need to make photocopies. The concept of checking out books seemed outdated to me. Thanks to my daughter's influence, I found myself obtaining a new library card and discovering that there were limits on how many books I could borrow as a new cardholder, along with other restrictions for provisional library card holders. I must applaud all the moms and dads who spend quality time in the library with their kids. It's like patiently waiting for your wife to finish shopping at an outlet mall. The bench may be cold and uncomfortable, but witnessing the sparkle in her eyes and the smile on her face as she enters and exits every store prevents from going completely insane for a little while longer. For Lauren, the local library was akin to Chuck E. Cheese's, with free coins (books) scattered everywhere.

Chapter 2

Rock'n Roll

When Lauren was in 2nd grade, she displayed an eagerness to join her older classmates' ranks. She was a clever child, always seeking new experiences. One day, while playing in the sandbox with other children, a boy carelessly threw a small rock that struck Lauren. Unfazed, she immediately confronted the boy and informed the playground monitor about the incident. Soon, they were both summoned to the principal's office to address the situation.

As the principal inquired about what had transpired, the boy claimed that it was an accidental occurrence, and that Lauren was making a fuss about nothing. However, Lauren vehemently asserted that the rock's impact was far from accidental; it was intentional. The principal, intrigued, asked Lauren how she could be certain of the boy's intentions. In response, Lauren calmly explained that if it had truly been an accident, the boy would have immediately approached her, asking, "Are you okay? I'm sorry." The fact that he hadn't done so reinforced Lauren's belief that it was not a mere accident.

Consequently, the boy received a detention for his actions, while Lauren was cleared of any wrongdoing. Several weeks later, during a PTA meeting, the principal shared this incident with me, giving me insight into Lauren's assertiveness and her ability to discern the truth.

Chapter 3

Skipping a Grade

Due to my wife's job being over 60 miles away from the school, I found myself taking on the role of a "school mom." While there's nothing wrong with a stay-at-home dad fulfilling that responsibility (despite having a full-time job of my own), it was a rarity to see an Asian student with the traditional mom and dad roles switched in our school.

Initially, I didn't mind blending in with the other parents during drop-offs and pick-ups. However, everything changed when Lauren's exceptional abilities started to shine, and she expressed a strong desire to become more involved in school activities. While all the moms were familiar with who I was, I only knew a few of them.

The after-school activities became quite burdensome for me. From dancing to swimming, soccer to music, theater performances, and more, the range of extracurricular commitments felt overwhelming.

I believed that having my daughter skip a whole grade would fulfill her academic needs and provide her with the right level of challenge in the near future. She consistently demonstrated a higher level of maturity compared to her peers and often interacted with third graders due to the small size of the school. While my wife and I had no doubts about Lauren's academic abilities, we were concerned about her physical and emotional development if she were to skip a grade.

To address our concerns, my wife and I discussed the matter with the principal, guidance counselor, and Lauren's current second grade teacher. They all agreed that Lauren would thrive academically if she skipped a grade. Considering her clear extroverted behavior and her excellent track record with new challenges, they were confident in her ability to adapt. However, what they didn't explicitly mention was that the final decision ultimately rested with us as parents, as long as it didn't have any negative consequences for them.

Before you judge, let me clarify that these administrators and teachers are competent professionals. I was simply naive to assume that the school environment would be vastly different from my workplace. Just like any workplace, schools follow Standard Operating Procedures (SOPs). They may tell you what you want to hear as long as all the necessary checkboxes are checked.

First, I had to write a memo to the principal informing them of our intention to have my child participate in a whole-grade acceleration study. Lauren's current grade teacher and a guidance counselor were required to submit similar letters to the State Gifted Education Board, with the principal's approval.

Second, the State Gifted Education Board would conduct multiple tests to determine if the individual was fully qualified. These tests would include assessments of IQ,

EQ, standard schoolwork (reading and math), and additional character evaluations.

Third, an IEP (Individualized Education Program) team was formed specifically for our child, and they developed a detailed plan to map out their educational journey.

Sounds promising, right? Well, despite completing all the necessary steps, the whole-grade acceleration did not happen. Almost half a year had passed, and we were still awaiting the final decision. Both our child and I became frustrated with the lengthy and complicated procedures involved.

Every time I spoke to someone from the Student Assistance Team (SAT), there were new tests or paperwork requirements that arose, and we were left waiting for someone in authority to sign off on the necessary documents.

They mentioned a case of a child in town who had previously skipped a grade but ended up disliking the new grade. As a result, they decided to reverse the decision and return to their previous grade, but things didn't go well for them on the playground. This conversation sparked a realization for me.

So, this is what I wrote and Lauren skipped a grade in the following week:

To: Mr. B███ and SAT Committee members

Subject: Request for Grade Advancement

Dear Mr. B███ and SAT Committee members,

I am writing to inform you of our decision to have Lauren participate in the 4th grade class starting from 17th February 2015. We believe that she is ready for new challenges and would like to provide her with the opportunity to advance into the next grade level.

While we have been patiently awaiting a response regarding the LCPS advance program, there has been no progress thus far. Recently, we discovered that even after additional testing, there are numerous additional steps and waiting involved before a decision is made by the LCPS. This process could potentially take another year to complete. Therefore, we have come to the conclusion that it would be wise to allow our daughter to join the 4th grade class now.

I want to emphasize that Ms. V██, Ms. D█████, and I have thoroughly discussed and considered the pros and cons of grade acceleration. We are fully aware of the potential impact it may have on Lauren's future. I would like to clarify that this decision is solely ours (Andrew To and Regina To). Ms. V██ and Ms. D█████ did not persuade us to take this course of action for our daughter to immediately join the 4th grade class.

Please be aware that we take full responsibility for any negative outcomes that may arise during this transition. Furthermore, we believe that assigning Ms. D█████ the additional task of generating and overseeing advanced materials for my daughter would be burdensome and unfair to her current students. We understand that this decision will have an impact on Lauren's academic, physical, and emotional growth. Although it was not an easy or hasty decision, the fact that Lauren strongly desires to accelerate to the next grade level and already has established friendships with 4th graders through the YS (Youth Center in W████) program has helped solidify our choice.

We acknowledge the risks associated with making this change midway through the 2014-2015 school year. However, we firmly believe that this decision will ultimately benefit Lauren more than waiting for another year to pass. Thus far, everyone involved agrees that Lauren should be given serious consideration for grade advancement. I look forward to receiving your response at your earliest convenience.

Respectfully,

Andrew To

I often come across the concept of CYA (Cover Your Actions/*Rear) in my workplace. I frequently find myself emailing important information to myself or copying related parties so that if any uncomfortable situations arise in the future, I have documented evidence to support my side. I've done this countless times.

It's perplexing to me why I didn't think of employing this strategy when the whole-grade acceleration process began.

Teachers and administrators are often apprehensive about the potential for lawsuits and being held accountable in every situation. Even if they have diligently followed all protocols and checked all the necessary boxes, they can easily lose their hard-earned experience, money, and respect overnight for something they never anticipated or asked for. Any deviation from their normal duties carries a certain degree of risk. It is also understandable that they cannot explicitly request a CYA letter or commitment.

It is common for us to seek someone or something to blame when things don't go our way. I am guilty of doing this myself, as it provides convenience and an easy way out. It becomes a habit to shift responsibility away from ourselves. We often hear Albert Einstein's definition of insanity: doing the same thing repeatedly and expecting different results. When any process stalls for any reason, it is crucial to take a step back, examine the bigger picture, and consider all the parties involved.

Chapter 4

PTA Meetings

If you have never attended a PTA meeting, I strongly encourage you to attend at least once. On paper, the purpose is to meet your child's teacher and principal prior to the first parent-teacher meeting and become familiar with school-related matters. However, in reality, the lack of relevance in these meetings can contribute to disengagement. If you're interested in learning about local milk cap savings that can help the school save 3 cents per cap, then you're in the right meeting. Unfortunately, as fathers, we often feel that PTA meetings are predominantly attended by mothers and that the discussions primarily revolve around topics traditionally associated with maternal roles.

Nevertheless, I still encourage you to attend a PTA meeting at least once. I recall a memorable incident during a PTA meeting when a fellow co-worker bravely stood up and posed a thought-provoking question to her 1st-grade teacher. She asked what measures the teacher was willing to take to provide adequate challenges for her exceptionally bright child, who struggled to stay engaged. The teacher's reaction mirrored the surprise felt by the rest of us in the room. It was a powerful reminder of the importance of actively participating in such meetings and advocating for your child's needs.

Anyway, in my opinion, the primary purpose of a Parent-Teacher Association (PTA) is often centered around fund-raising and financial support. Whether it's referred to as a booster club, a fundraiser, assistance for sports activities, funding for field trips, or even enhancing the school's landscaping, it typically revolves around generating funds for the school's needs.

So, what would be the most effective way to raise funds for these purposes? Engaging in activities like collecting milk bottle caps or selling magazines that nobody reads may not yield significant results.

Similarly, expecting parents to break their backs with car washes may not yield considerable results. Indeed, there are many more effective ways to raise money, such as selling hotdogs, sodas, and water during school or city events. Pre-selling enchilada plates can also generate better results compared to labor-intensive car washes. These food-related fundraising activities can attract a larger customer base and potentially generate higher profits for the cause.

To me, the best way to raise money for the school is to elect the right PTA president. Yes. Choose the right PTA president! A capable leader can bring innovative fundraising ideas, mobilize the community, and ensure effective fundraising for various purposes.

Thanks to my higher education experience at a Big Ten school, I learned a few tricks for securing funding. One instance that stands out is when I was invited to an orientation party organized by the Chinese Students Association, despite having no affiliation with Chinese culture. My class-mate invited me, mentioning that there would be free food.

Attending the party provided me with an opportunity to observe the techniques employed by the Chinese Students Association to raise funds.

When I arrived at the orientation party, they were wel-coming freshmen and preparing for a softball game between the freshmen and upperclassmen. It wasn't an entirely new concept, but it added some fun to the event. However, be-fore the game began, an unexpected group of white ladies showed up to throw the first pitch and take some honorary pictures.

The presence of these unexpected white ladies at the Chinese Students Association event might have seemed surprising at first glance. However, they were actually mem-bers of the university book club, led by the wife of the university president. It is possible that they were invited as special guests or as community members who wanted to demonstrate their support for the association and its activi-ties. In events like these, it is common to extend invitations to guests from diverse backgrounds, aiming to promote in-clusivity and encourage cultural exchange.

Their involvement in the event, including the ceremonial first pitch and the honorary pictures taken, could serve various purposes, such as securing sponsorships and dona-tions. It is likely that they were able to secure donations from local businesses, particularly those with connections to the Chinese community. These businesses may have contributed funds in exchange for recognition or advertis-ing opportunities during the event.

Indeed, the PTA has the potential to establish partner-ships and collaborations with local businesses, as well as national companies, to sponsor school organizations, sports teams, or cultural clubs. Such collaborations offer numerous mutual benefits, including cost-sharing, enhancing the company's image, and the opportunity to reach a wider audience. This ultimately increases the likelihood of generating more funds, eliminating the need for laborious fundraisers. No more back-breaking car wash PTA!

Chapter 5

Daycare

I also have a 14-year-old boy who is quite ordinary. Perhaps that's how I wanted to raise him, though I'm not entirely certain. Andrew is two years younger than his older sister Lauren, and the two of them possess completely different personalities.

When they were infants, enrolling both children in full-day daycare proved to be quite challenging, to say the least. Actually, calling it "tough" might be an understatement. It was incredibly difficult, especially considering that our monthly daycare expenses surpassed our mortgage payments. Unfortunately, we had limited options for daycare services since our closest relatives lived in Boston. Additionally, their mother was a full-time nursing student, and I had to commute over 60 miles each day.

One day, I received a phone call from the daycare informing me that my child was unwell and that I needed to pick him up as soon as possible. Concerned, I asked for details about what had happened. They explained that Andrew had experienced three loose stools within a short span of time, but there was no accompanying fever. According to the day-care's policy, they notify parents to pick up their child after two loose stools occur.

Immediately, I scheduled an emergency check-up appointment with our pediatrician and took Andrew in for examination. After a thorough assessment, our pediatrician found no signs of dehydration or any obvious indications of illness. However, he advised us to monitor for any further episodes of loose stools or the onset of a fever. Other than that, he assured us that Andrew was healthy and able to return to daycare the following day.

Andrew had remained healthy with no signs of any loose stools since I picked him up, so I was prepared to drop him off at daycare the next day. However, I was informed that it had not been more than 24 hours since I had picked him up, so I couldn't utilize the care that I was paying for. Despite the doctor clearing Andrew to return, the daycare policy held more weight than the professional opinion of a board-certified pediatrician. There was no point in arguing with the front desk staff as they were simply following the rules. However, I felt compelled to speak up for what I believed in, as this situation could affect not only me but others as well.

As a result, I wrote a letter expressing my concerns, and the daycare revised its policy the following week.

From: Y. Andrew To Date: 05 December 2008 To: D███ M. R███████

Subject: 04 December 2008: Letter/CYS Management

Ms. R███████/CYS Management,

I would like to express my gratitude for your prompt response to my email. I understand that you strive to address the concerns of dissatisfied parents in a timely and responsible manner, seeking the best possible solution for both parents and CYS. I want to emphasize that my intention was not to file a complaint to upset your staff or the caretakers. My main purpose was to seek clarification regarding the vague policy of Child Youth and School Service and its potential consequences.

Firstly, I want to commend your professionalism, which was evident when I learned that you have already taken steps to amend the policy in order to minimize or eliminate instances of poor judgment, as we discussed during our phone conversation last night.

I also acknowledge and respect your objective of ensuring a healthy environment for those who are in good health. As a parent, I prioritize the well-being of my children and greatly appreciate a safe and healthy environment. However, when a child in a decent condition is sent home, it raises questions.

I am not doubting the caretaker's report. I was informed that Andrew had three loose stools within a span of five hours, but Andrew appears to be extremely healthy with no signs of any issues. This was also confirmed last night during the visit to the physician's office at RGMC. It is frustrating to encounter doubt regarding the nature of the visit after the examination. Since I picked him up from daycare, Andrew has had four diaper changes, yet there have been no signs of loose stools. This clearly demonstrates the poor judgment in releasing him yesterday and not accepting him today (Baby Andrew is at home today due to the 24-hour policy).

However, I will not pursue any further inquiries on this matter. I willingly and respectfully adhere to your policy. I acknowledge the sincerity of your response and appreciate all of your efforts.

Once again, I have immense respect and trust in your Child Youth and School Service due to your demonstrated dedication and sense of urgency in every situation I have encountered with you. I firmly believe that your staff and caretakers exhibit exceptional professionalism. I sincerely hope that the complaint I have raised does not affect the future of my two children at your center.

Respectfully,

Andrew To

After sending this email, the School Service Director and I developed a good rapport and became friends. I also took on the role of President of the Child Youth Parent Representative to advocate for other parents' concerns. Initially, I had some apprehension about how my young child would be treated following the confrontation. However, I firmly believe that change can only happen if action is taken. It is important to believe that if we do nothing, nothing will change.

Chapter 6

Kid Jay

Andrew had a classmate named Jay, a tall Hispanic boy with a beautiful smile. However, Jay has already repeated two years in school. One day, Andrew came to me and shared a story about Jay. He explained how Jay had stepped in to help a smaller kid who was being bullied by another student. Unfortunately, Jay ended up getting in trouble because the teacher did not believe his side of the story, until Andrew stood up and recounted what he had witnessed that day.

I felt an immense sense of pride in my son's actions, and it made me curious about Jay's circumstances. Andrew often mentioned that Jay was struggling academically. Whenever Jay made a mistake on a question, he would proclaim to everyone that he was stupid. Despite his teacher's reassurances that he wasn't, Jay chose to believe otherwise.

I understood that this negative self-perception was a defense mechanism Jay had developed to protect himself from the judgments of others. Thoughts like "I am not good enough" or "I am stupid" can significantly impact one's future. I was concerned that Jay's attitude would hinder his progress as he grew older. Since Jay and Andrew were still young, I believed it was too early for Jay to give up. That's why I encouraged Andrew to become close friends with Jay, hoping that their friendship would have a positive influence on Jay's self-perception and future growth.

I understood that even at a young age, children have a sense of self-pride that shapes their character. I also recognized that Jay's negative self-talk served as a false shield against potential judgments from others.

I advised my son Andrew to discover Jay's strengths first. We wanted to ensure that Jay could assist Andrew with something he excelled in before Andrew offered his help with schoolwork. It turned out to be an effective approach. Andrew expressed to Jay that he needed a true and supportive friend who would stand up for him, especially when others doubted him. Jay was pleased to hear this and they became good friends. Initially, Jay wasn't particularly enthusiastic when Andrew offered to help him with multiplication tables, but things changed over the following weeks.

Interestingly, this experience benefited Andrew more than Jay. Andrew learned the value of friendship and the joy that comes from helping others. I was thrilled to see my son gain this valuable lesson, knowing that it would stay with him for a long time.

Chapter 7

Middle School

This brings me back to a significant chapter of my life during early middle school. To put it in perspective, I wasn't born in this country, but I eagerly arrived here as soon as the opportunity arose. My family belongs to the category of legal immigrants.

Now, I'm not referring to the earlier waves of Irish and Italian immigrants who arrived decades ago. Instead, our story as immigrants from Asia began in the late 80s. It all started when my aunt married an American soldier back in the 60s, opening the doors for her relatives to join her and settle in this new land. Although this particular method of legal immigration has since been abolished, it held considerable popularity during the 80s.

Our journey as immigrants began when our application was filed in the mid-70s. However, due to the nature of our preferred immigrant category, which ranked lower in urgency (category 4), it took an arduous wait of over 17 years before our grant was finally issued in the late 80s. Throughout this time, we invested substantial amounts of money in processing fees, adding to the challenges we faced along the way.

Because of my personal experience as a legal immigrant, my perspective on the issue of illegal immigration at the border differs significantly from that of the typical minority residing here. I will delve deeper into this topic in a later chapter of this book.

One vivid memory that stands out is when I first arrived at San Francisco airport. A person, likely an immigration officer, handed me a document to sign, and without hesitation, I inscribed my name in Korean. Little did I know at the time that this seemingly simple act would become my signature on the permanent green card, symbolizing my official status as a lawful resident.

Throughout the years, the design and appearance of the permanent green card have undergone several transformations. Initially, it was indeed a green-colored card, quite literally living up to its name. I became aware of this fact when my second sister worked at a bank in Philadelphia and encountered an elderly lady who presented her original green card for identification purposes. However, as time passed, subsequent versions of the green card transitioned to a white-colored base, differentiating them from the original green iteration.

These changes in the appearance of the green card reflect the evolving nature of immigration policies and the documentation associated with them.

Returning to the topic of the green card, it is worth noting that our "not so green" card was, in fact, a truly permanent document. Unlike the newer versions, our green card did not bear an expiration date. It served as indefinite proof of our lawful residency status. However, I should clarify that the current iteration of the permanent green card does come with an expiration period of either 2 or 10 years. This means that individuals who possess the new permanent green card must undergo the process of renewal if they wish to maintain their legal status and continue residing here.

The introduction of an expiration date on the green card raises questions about its perceived permanence. While the term "permanent" may still be used to describe it, the inclusion of an expiration period suggests a shift in the concept. It seems that the designation of "permanent" has become more nuanced and requires periodic reaffirmation of one's legal status. This change reflects the evolving immigration landscape and the need for more consistent updates and reviews of individuals' residency documentation.

As an immigrant who experienced the earlier version of the green card, I find this transition intriguing. It prompts contemplation about the shifting nature of immigration policies and the expectations placed upon individuals to actively maintain their legal status, even with a document that was once considered "permanent."

Chapter 8

Bob and Doug

My first day of middle school in the United States remains etched in my memory as an unforgettable experience. Everything seemed enormous to me, from the size of the people to the chairs, desks, and whiteboards in the classrooms. Even something as simple as a meatball sandwich presented a challenge—I could only manage to eat two out of the three small meatballs. It's amusing to reflect on that now, considering I can easily devour a two-foot-long Subway meatball sandwich without breaking a sweat.

Not only were the physical aspects larger, but the overall scale of everything amazed me. The kids around me seemed much bigger than what I was accustomed to, and the teachers appeared like towering figures. The classrooms themselves were three to four times larger than those in my previous school, providing ample space for learning. I was in awe of the vast soccer and baseball fields, adorned with lush green grass instead of the dirt I was accustomed to back home. To top it all off, there was even a swimming pool—an unexpected bonus that added an extra touch of excitement to my new school environment.

During those early days, my first American friends were Bob and Doug. Though I can't recall their last names now, the sense of camaraderie we shared at Keith Valley Middle School in 1989 made it a remarkable and incredibly cool place to be. The memories and experiences from that time have left a lasting impression on me, serving as a testament to the vibrant and dynamic nature of my early years in the United States.

Bob and Doug, whose names coincidentally translated to "rice" and "rice cake" in Korean, provided me with some hilarious moments during my early days in the United States. Despite not knowing much English at the time, their repeated references to rice and rice cake never failed to make me chuckle. We would laugh together, even though Bob and Doug probably had no clue why I found it so amusing. Nevertheless, they were good friends, and our shared experiences created a strong bond. After all, why wouldn't rice get along with rice cake? Thinking back on those days, I can't help but feel a sense of nostalgia and fondness. Bob and Doug, if you ever come across this, know that I miss you guys and cherish the memories we made together.

Chapter 9

Superintendent

All of my children were born and raised in this beautiful country, and I am grateful for the opportunities that all my kids and I have been given. It was the support and sacrifices of their grandparents that enabled me to provide these opportunities for my children as well.

I proudly served in the U.S. Army and was honorably discharged over 20 years ago. Despite transitioning to civilian life, I continue to serve as an engineer, contributing to the betterment of this nation in my own capacity.

However, there are occasions when individuals approach me and attempt to undermine or belittle me because of my accent, which I have learned is impossible to completely eliminate. In such instances, I confidently remind them of their place and assert my own worth and contributions to society.

Our home school district offers a Bilingual Multicultural Education Program, which I discovered in the most unexpected manner. When we initially registered for school after Lauren was born, we were required to check the box indicating that all family members spoke English at home. However, when we registered Andrew for school, we had to check the box indicating that my wife and I speak to each other in Korean. Little did we know the challenges this would bring us in the years that followed.

This Bilingual Multicultural Education Program is designed to utilize two languages, namely English and the student's home or heritage language, as the medium of instruction in the teaching and learning process. Sounds good so far right?

I want to clarify the purpose of the program. The main objective of this program is to provide valuable support to bilingual students who come from diverse cultural and linguistic backgrounds, enabling them to excel in an English-speaking public school environment and facilitating their effective understanding of learning instructions. The program aims to create an inclusive and supportive educational environment that recognizes and values the unique strengths and challenges of these students, helping them thrive academically and linguistically.

However, it appears that in reality, the program may inadvertently label Spanish-speaking students and group them together, potentially leading to negative stereotypes. This could create a perception that these students are being used as a means to obtain additional funding from the state, rather than genuinely addressing their educational needs.

How did I find out all of this? I came across a public readme buried within the school policy, where I read all 38 pages detailing the purpose of this program.

My concerns regarding the program arose when I inquired about language support for a student like Andrew, who may speak a language other than English or Spanish.

In Andrew's case, he does not speak or understand Korean. To my surprise, I discovered that the program only offers support in Spanish and lacks resources for other languages. This lack of inclusivity raises concerns about the program's effectiveness in meeting the needs of students from diverse language backgrounds, such as Andrew, who may require assistance in a language other than Spanish. It is important to ensure that language support programs cater to the unique needs of all students, regardless of their specific language backgrounds.

I became particularly upset when Andrew, who is fluent in English, was wrongly identified as a bilingual student. Bilingual programs are typically designed to support students who speak a language other than English at home, aiding them in acquiring English proficiency while maintaining their native language skills. It is essential to recognize that Andrew did not fall into this category, and I made sure to communicate this to the school. However, despite my efforts, it seems that my concerns were disregarded by the school administration.

The school informed me that Andrew did not pass an English proficiency test. So he will be placed into this special group of students. I was extremely surprised by this revelation because Andrew has always been an A student and has never encountered any difficulties with English.

In response to this situation, I decided to write a letter to the superintendent, expressing my concerns and seeking clarification. However, a remarkable turn of events occurred the following week in Andrew's case.

Subject: Formal Complaint Regarding Request from LCPS and ███████ School Principal

Dear Superintendent Dr. E███,

I am writing this email to formally complain about the nonsensical request made by Ms. M█████, the principal of ████████ School, on behalf of LCPS. Her rude, unprofessional, and disrespectful attitude towards concerned parents has left me deeply disappointed.

Last Friday (September 29, 2017), my wife and I were contacted by Ms. M█████ regarding the signing of a certain bilingual document for our child, Andrew. She emphasized the urgency of the matter and insisted that my immediate attention was required. According to her, I had previously signed this document, but they were unable to locate the signed copy, thus necessitating my signature again.

Having been a part of the LCPS system for a while, we are aware that last-minute requests of this nature from the school are rare. Previous principals rarely made such demands of parents. Unfortunately, I was not available at W██████ that Friday as I was off, and my wife was working in ██████. I informed Ms. M████ that if my child could bring the papers home, I would review and sign them, returning them to her by Monday. However, upon reading the papers, I discovered that they were not the same as those I had signed on May 1, 2017.

On Monday morning (October 2, 2017), I scheduled an appointment with Ms. M████s and had a meeting with her, a representative from the LCPS bilingual department (via speakerphone), and myself. During the meeting, I made it explicitly clear that my child is not bilingual and only speaks English at home.

However, the representative from the bilingual department insisted that any student whose parents check the box indicating a language other than English spoken at home must undergo a proficiency test and be evaluated accordingly. I expressed my disagreement with this assessment, finding it ridiculous. Furthermore, I felt that this amounted to discrimination since my child is a perfectly proficient native English speaker. I also made it clear that he is only proficient in one language.

How can a student be subjected to testing and evaluation simply because their parents speak different languages to each other? My child was born and raised here, excelling in classwork. Are you suggesting that the LCPS curriculum is less important than a trivial language test administered to my child? And where are the test results? Was my permission sought for my child's participation in this special test?

Throughout these conversations, Ms. M████ constantly interrupted me, displaying rude facial gestures and unprofessional behavior. To make matters worse, she signed the document right in front of me, claiming that I had refused to sign it, so she took the liberty of signing it herself. This response is simply unbelievable.

When I requested further explanation after the meeting with the three individuals, Ms. M████ simply replied that I should schedule another appointment for another meeting.

I understand that school principals are busy individuals, just as I am. I currently hold a professional position in W████████, and my time is also valuable.

This incident clearly indicates that Ms. M████ shows no interest in my child's future and exhibits a "don't care" attitude. We are aware that you are a very busy individual with many other students to look after. We also understand that you have recently become aware of this situation and may not have had much time to fully understand the discussions that have taken place.

I kindly request that you follow up on this matter and inform us of what can be done to ensure a better process moving forward.

Thank you for your attention to this issue.

Andrew To

After sending the letter, LCPS promptly contacted me to address my concerns. We arranged a meeting to discuss the issue, and during our discussion, it came to light that none of the middle school students, including Andrew, who were labeled as "bilingual," had actually not completed the English proficiency test. It was revealed that this was primarily due to their desire to start recess early, as the unplanned test was not participated in by all the students.

To demonstrate the seriousness of this event to me and my family, I decided to bring along a close friend Allen who happens to be tall, physically imposing, and Caucasian. I informed Allen not to engage in any conversation but rather to simply listen and take notes for me. My intention was to have an additional witness present during the meeting with the school district superintendent's office. However, it is disheartening to hear that the superintendent's personnel seemed more concerned about Allen's presence and repeatedly questioned whether he was an attorney from a law firm, despite his clear statement that he is not a practicing attorney.

I want to clarify that my friend's role was solely to provide support and act as a witness to the proceedings. While his physical presence may have made an impact, it is essential to focus on the issue at hand rather than dwell on his appearance or background. The primary goal should always be to find a resolution and ensure the well-being and safety of all students and families within the school district.

As a result, the school arranged for them to complete the test, and to our delight, Andrew passed with flying colors.

Interestingly, it was discovered that most of the students labeled as "bilingual" had minimal or no proficiency in Spanish at all, despite the program being advertised as such. This revelation further highlighted the misclassification of students and the inadequacy of the program in identifying and assisting those who genuinely require language support.

I am deeply concerned about the potential unfair placement of Hispanic and other minority students in programs or their classification as special groups within the school system, without receiving the necessary additional support they may require. It is disheartening to witness the use of minority groups as pawns within our current educational system, especially considering that many parents may lack the resources or ability to advocate effectively for their children.

It is crucial that we address this issue and ensure that all students, regardless of their background, are treated fairly and given equal opportunities. Every student deserves an education that supports their individual needs and encourages their academic and personal growth. As a community, we should work together to create a school system that values diversity, promotes inclusivity, and provides the necessary support for all students to thrive.

Chapter 10

Kristen

Kristeen was the correct spelling that I submitted as her name when the state birth certificate folks stopped by the hospital when Kristen was born. However, my wife Regina decided to drop one 'e' because she did not like the sound of 'teen' in our baby's name at the last minute.

Well, we still call her Kristeen but it's just spelled Kristen now.

Lucky for me, the daycare on the Army base offered parents the option to read articles and provide summary reports, which would give me a huge 10% discount on fees every month. So, I started doing that for a while, and it turned out to be beneficial. I learned a few tricks from those articles that I still apply today.

One of the valuable tricks I learned is to spend individual time with each of my kids. I give each child a special secret or experience that is unique to them. Being budget-conscious, I take each child separately to the dollar store, where they can choose something special that they don't have to share with their siblings. It's a small yet meaningful way to create individual connections and make each child feel special.

Understanding the needs of your children is crucial as it serves as the key to successful parenting. By studying and learning about your kids' individual requirements, you can better meet their needs and provide them with the necessary support and guidance. This knowledge empowers you to make informed decisions and create an environment that fosters their growth, happiness, and overall well-being.

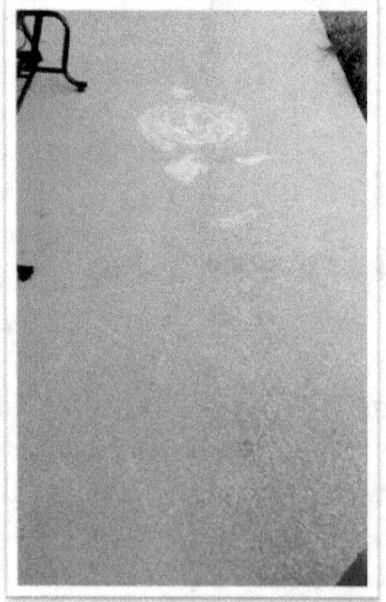

Chapter 11

Magic

I must admit, it had never occurred to me that not all grade schools in the United States allowed parents to have lunch with their kids. However, I was pleasantly surprised to learn that at Lauren, Andrew, and Kristen's school, such visits were warmly welcomed. It was heartening to see that when a parent had the chance to visit, they generously allowed up to two friends to join the lunch group and provided a separate table for the occasion. This unique opportunity became a highly sought-after experience for the kids, creating an atmosphere of excitement and antici-pation whenever a parent would come to join the lunchtime festivities.

As a devoted parent, I embraced the role of the "school mom" and aimed to make the most of these precious moments with my children and their friends. I remember the first time I joined Lauren's lunch; her outgoing nature and popularity among her peers were evident as everyone eagerly hoped to be chosen to sit with her. However, I found it quite challenging to keep the group engaged with my stories, as their attention was split between the excitement of the occasion and their desire to interact with their chosen friends.

Later, as Andrew reached the age where he too wanted me to visit, I noticed that he didn't have as many demands from friends to sit with him as Lauren did. Nonetheless, the lunchtime experience took an unexpected turn when I stumbled upon a series of intriguing coin tricks on YouTube. It was a moment of serendipity that changed the dynamics completely. Before I knew it, the word had spread like wildfire throughout the entire school, and I had gained the endearing title of "magic tricks dad." The kids started eagerly asking Andrew to pick them even before my scheduled visits, and their enthusiasm and joy were evident each time we gathered for lunch. I must admit, it was a delightful experience to be known as the "magic tricks dad" and to see the smiles on the children's faces as I performed my repertoire of tricks for them.

By the time Kristen's turn came around for a school lunch date, her friends had already formed an image of me as a full-time magician, which added an extra layer of excitement and anticipation. Their enthusiasm was so infectious that I began receiving open invitations to other kids' birthday parties, further solidifying the bond I had formed with the school community.

As a parent actively involved in my kids' school life, I couldn't be more fulfilled by the positive impact I had on fostering excitement, camaraderie, and friendship among the children. These special lunchtime gatherings not only created lasting memories for my own children but also contributed to the overall positive atmosphere within the school. Being able to share my time and talents with the kids and witnessing their genuine joy and appreciation made every effort worthwhile, and I cherished each moment spent as the "magic tricks dad" in their eyes.

Chapter 12

Godmother

When Kristen was born, we didn't have to search for godparents because Lauren and Andrew's godmother was already watching over her.

You may have heard the saying, "It takes a village to raise a child," and indeed, there are times when two parents alone may not be enough. Every helping hand makes a difference. I am in awe of single parents who manage to raise a child on their own—it truly is a miracle to me.

Over the past 20 years, Lori has continued to embrace my children as her own, offering unwavering love and support. Her nurturing presence has been a constant source of stability in their lives, guiding them during times when I couldn't be there. The care she has shown them is truly priceless and has played a significant role in shaping their growth and development.

I often contemplate the possibility that there may come a time when my two girls need to discuss something they may not feel comfortable sharing with Mom and Dad. While

I hope such a situation never arises, it's important for them to know they have someone to confide in. Providing them with additional trustworthy choices ensures they have the support they need as they grow up. Having more positive influences in their lives can only be a beneficial aspect of their upbringing.

If you don't have anyone like our godmother, it's not too late to search for one. It's much easier for you to become good godparents, and the new family will soon become part of your family.

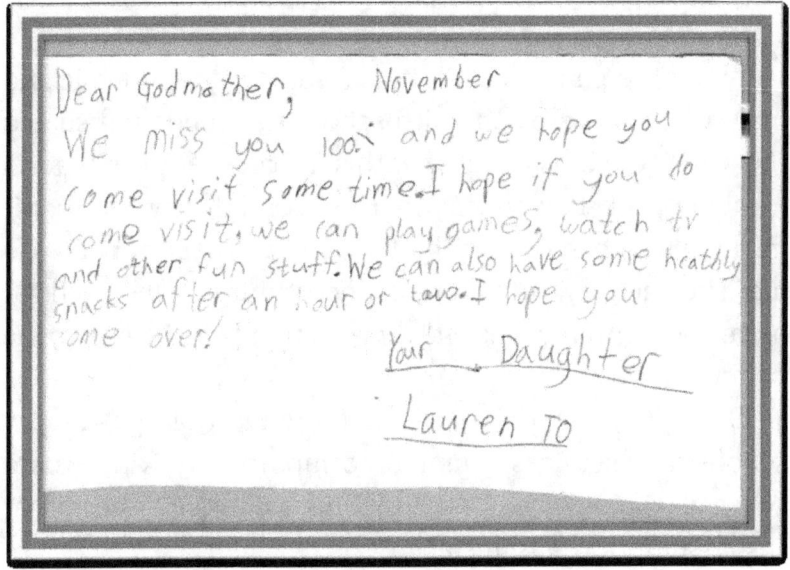

Chapter 13

Bowling Alley

When the pandemic hit, it caused widespread panic and uncertainty. As a parent with school-age children, I shared the same concerns about how this unprecedented situation would impact their education. However, I discovered that it might have been one of the best things that happened to me. The pandemic provided an opportunity for me to spend more time with my kids and allowed them to open up to me in new ways.

Once, I made the naive assumption that paying for school-care services/ summer camp for my kids would cover all their needs. However, I have come to realize that this assumption was mistaken.

I learned the hard way that the school-care services/ summer camp for my kids didn't cover all the expenses. They often went on mid-week trips to places like the bowling alley, local zoo, or Bob-o's family fun center. While the fees for bowling, zoo admission, and Bob-o's basic coins were included, I didn't realize that other kids brought their own money for snacks and additional playing tokens. Whenever my son Andrew asked for money for these events, I consistently said no, unaware of the situation. Looking back, I feel cheap, neglectful, and like a bad father. I wish he had explained it to me more clearly so that I could have understood the situation better. In reality, how can I expect my kids to explain something when their dad has already made up his mind? When faced with a situation where I've already formed a strong opinion, it can be challenging to expect young Andrew to explain something that contradicts or challenges his father's perspective.

The realization of this during the pandemic has been a painful experience for me.

When I finally asked Andrew's older sibling Lauren if that's what was happening during those programs, she admitted that it was all true. However, she knew my answer would be firm, so she always found ways to secretly bring money for the events. On the other hand, Andrew, even though he had his own spending money, obediently followed my instructions and watched others from the sidelines. Andrew's honesty made me extremely proud, but it also revealed that he lacks flexibility in such situations.

On the last day of their bowling alley trip, Andrew told me that the manager gave him fries and ice cream for free because he felt sorry that Andrew was the only one in the group who never bought anything. Hearing this broke my heart.

It's disheartening to realize that I unintentionally became an insensitive father.

Fortunately, thanks to Andrew's intervention, Kristen now has a $20 bill every time she attends those events. I've made it a point to ensure that Kristen uses some of that money to buy snacks or playing coins for her friends who may have forgotten to bring their own.

Chapter 14

Mercedes, Baby! Mercedes!

Do you know why riding a roller coaster is so much fun? It's because it offers a thrilling experience with its varying speeds, changes in direction, and unexpected drops and twists. The roller coaster's dynamic nature creates a sense of excitement and anticipation.

Sometimes, I believe that my God ensures that his creations have the opportunity to enjoy these rides until the time when you meet him again.

I once had a co-worker named Billy who was not only a friend but also an incredibly wise individual. It took over a decade for him to reveal his true feelings toward me because he is an exceptionally cautious person.

He became a mentor, guiding me towards personal growth, professional growth, and helping me become a better version of myself. Billy consistently reminded me to invest effort in my marriage, even during times when everything seemed to be going smoothly.

He often used his own personal example to inspire me and emphasized the importance of seizing opportunities for growth and positive change in the present moment. His stories served as a reminder that I don't necessarily need a second chance to make meaningful progress in my life. I am truly grateful for his guidance and the profound impact he had on shaping my perspective and actions.

> + 찬미 예수
>
> 세상에서 젤 멋진 내남편
> " I Love you so much !
> The day has arrived when you turn one more year older. I hope we laugh and cry and we always have each other shoulders."
>
> Happy Birthday honey !!
>
> 늘 말로 표현해서 보여주진 못했지만
> 결혼해서 지금까지 당신을 만날 수
> 있어서 너무 너무 행복해.
> 게으름과 냄새 정도 단점들
> 100점 만점에 100점의 남편,
> Lauren + Andrew 의 아빠, 큰아들
> 큰사위. 남동생. 형. 형부. 형님 그리고
> 멋진 남자인 도 영 찬 님의 생일을
> 다시한번 진심으로 축하 한다.
> 철없는 아내 때문에 많이 힘들지?
> 조금만 기둘려, 내가 직장만 구하면
> 우리 신랑 완전 호강시켜 줄테니깐..

Thanks to his suggestion, I decided to surprise my spouse, Regina, by purchasing two tickets to the Nutcracker ballet. However, since ballet performances typically don't involve dialogue and feature repeated music for over four hours (I did not know this at the time), the experience taught us that it wasn't quite the enjoyable night out we had anticipated. Oh, don't get me wrong. Some of you may truly enjoy the Nutcracker ballet.

The experience taught us the importance of spending quality time together, especially during challenging times. It reminded us that nurturing our relationship and creating meaningful memories are crucial when facing difficulties.

Regina is an experienced Registered Nurse (RN) who currently holds a highly respected position and earns a good income. However, her journey to reach this point was not always smooth or straightforward.

When our kids were little and money was tight, our plan was also tight. She became an RN and started contributing to our income for a better future. We took out numerous student loans, and she began her journey from the very beginning.

The home economics major degree from overseas seemed worthless, and she had to start from scratch, learning the "A, B, C" of her new journey - especially for a Pre-Nursing major, it requires a solid foundation in biology, chemistry, and math, along with additional English courses as needed.

She did remarkably well, and I also excelled as I had to assist her with a lot of writing tasks. We're a good team. Once she got accepted into nursing school, transitioning from her pre-nursing status, we both saw that the end of the tunnel was near. But we weren't prepared for the twists and turns of the next roller coaster. She failed her first class by a mere 0.03. I was certain they would round it up for her, but unfortunately, that didn't happen. We had to write a letter to the nursing school, pleading for one more chance to continue. As it turned out, every nursing school in the country allowed two chances to complete the degree, so she had one more opportunity.

I didn't have to remind her that she couldn't mess this up because she knew more than I did, but unfortunately, it happened. The following semester, she failed another class. This time, she was officially kicked out of nursing school. All those prerequisite classes and nursing courses we invested our time and money into were now gone.

Even our marriage was shaken. Disappointment permeated every aspect of our lives, and our conversations with each other were far from kind. What do we do now? Where do we go from here? Oh, yes, the student loans loomed over us as well.

I volunteered for every available overtime at work, which left me exhausted and filled with anger. I'm certain that my unkind words and actions also hurt Regina in many ways. In any case, things were not going very well during that time.

One Saturday during overtime, as I found myself in the post exchange store picking up my lunch, a familiar face caught my attention. It was none other than my old friend Andre Bullet. Andre, my longtime friend and colleague, is more than 10 years my senior, and we share a deep history together. In his past, he was a Division One football lineman, and he once mentioned that he appeared skinny during his playing days. However, from my perspective, he has always exuded a sense of being big and tall. Our bond is particularly unique as we are among the very few minority engineers working together, which has further strengthened our connection.

A few years ago, both Regina and I were invited to his youngest teen kids' birthday party, which allowed me to learn more about Andre's personal life. I discovered that his wife held a high-ranking director position in a prominent nursing firm. It was impressive to see her achieve such success in her career.

Andre looked at me with concern and asked, "Andrew, you don't look so well. What's going on, brother?" I sighed and mustered the courage to open up to him. "Well, Andre," I began, "it's embarrassing to talk about, but something unfortunate happened to Regina. She was actually kicked out of the nursing program because she failed two classes. I'm at a loss for what to do next."

Andre looked at me with a reassuring smile, understanding the weight of the situation. I knew he wasn't laughing at me; he was a true friend who genuinely cared. Before long, he opened up and shared his own experience with empathy. He revealed that his wife had faced a similar setback when she was a nursing student, having been kicked out of the program as well.

This revelation brought a sense of relief and comfort to me, knowing that we weren't alone in facing such challenges.

Curious about Andre's approach, I asked him, "So, what did you do, Andre? Did you unleash a storm of dominance?" Andre chuckled and shook his head. "No, my grasshopper," he replied. "Instead, I took my wife to the Mercedes-Benz dealership and bought her a new car". "Wait a minute, Andre," I exclaimed. "I don't think you heard me correctly. Regina failed the nursing school." Andre nodded knowingly and said, "Yes, I heard you correctly".

Andre wanted to show his wife that despite the setback, he believed in her and wanted her to persevere. Andre convinced her to gather the courage to go back and take on the challenge of a new nursing school.

I was taken aback by his response.

Andre's unconventional response left me intrigued. I couldn't help but wonder how buying a car and encouraging Regina to pursue another nursing program could possibly be the solution to her failure. Andre's personal story served as a reminder that setbacks can happen to anyone, and that there were paths to overcome them. It gave me hope and reassurance that we could navigate this difficult situation together.

I believed that this trip would not only help Regina unwind but also offer her a fresh perspective on life. Being in the presence of her parents and exploring the familiar yet unfamiliar surroundings of her childhood would create lasting memories for her and our children. It would allow her to reflect on her journey, find inspiration from her family's support, and gain a renewed sense of purpose.

너무 너무 사랑해!
2012년에도 우리 서로 터더더더
사랑하고, 감사하며 살자궁~♡
늘 건강챙기고, 늘 웃고, 늘 유모와
위트가 가득가득한 내 신랑이
태어난 날... 너무 너무 좋다. ♡

2011년 12월 20일
영찬이를 너무 사랑하는
규리...♡

Well, it works. Regina's success as Andre's wife and the Mercedes trick turned out to be the best advice to save my marriage and advance Regina's career. It's remarkable how a thoughtful gesture and unconventional approach can have such positive outcomes.

Chapter 15

Within Reach, yet Eternally Distant

It brings me joy every time my wife Regina visits her parents. However, there is a bittersweet aspect to it as well.

My grandmother's resting place is in Delaware, a significant distance from where I was born in Korea. Sadly, she passed away just a year after my birth, making it impossible for her to meet me, the first grandson of our family. My uncle has reiterated numerous times to my father that my grandmother had a strong desire to see me.

The year 1968 marked my parents' marriage in Korea, a time when they were facing financial hardships due to my father's modest income as a teacher. However, things took a turn for the better when my mother decided to open a small restaurant in Masan, which turned out to be a great success. Despite the challenges and sacrifices, my mother and grandmother shared a close and affectionate relationship during the time they lived together. Before my grandma departed from the state with my uncle, my mom made a heartfelt decision. She arranged for my grandma to visit her hometown and reunite with her family. This initiative stemmed from my mom learning that my grandma hadn't been able to return to her hometown since she married my grandpa, a period spanning almost 50 years. Upon discovering this, my mom felt compelled to provide my grandma with the opportunity to revisit her roots, reconnect with her relatives, and experience the familiarity of her hometown once again. Despite being less than 45 miles away from my home, it felt like an eternal distance for my grandma. In those days, there were no highways or proper roads in Korea, making the journey even more challenging and time-consuming.

Grandma was aware that both of her parents had passed away and she often wondered about her four older brothers. Sadly, it turned out that all of her brothers had also passed away. However, their children held fond memories of her. Even on their deathbeds, all of her brothers expressed concern for their younger sister and wondered how she was faring. It is worth noting that in traditional Korean old culture, when a girl gets married, she becomes a part of her husband's family and is expected to primarily focus on her new family. As a result, it is not customary for married women to frequently visit their original families unless specific circumstances dictate otherwise. My mom was incredibly thankful for organizing that visit, as it ultimately became my grandma's last cherished memory of her hometown. Additionally, my mom shared with me that during the visit, my grandma brought back two large bags of peanuts, a specialty of her hometown that my cousin had sent along with her. The city was renowned for its delectable peanuts, and my grandma wanted to share a taste of her hometown with our family.

Chapter 16

Dr. Notsowisedog

Last month, the graduating senior class of 2023 from all five local high schools in our district, who had graduated from WSMR Elementary School, gathered at WSMR Elementary School for a special event.

This cherished tradition allowed the graduating students to walk the halls of their former school, reconnect with their former teachers, engage with younger students, and share their plans for the summer and upcoming college years. Each student proudly donned the respected color associated with their respective high school gown. This annual event has been a longstanding tradition, fostering a sense of community and providing a meaningful opportunity for students to bid farewell to their beloved teachers and old friends before embarking on their college journeys. As someone from the East Coast, I yearn for such events in my region, as they offer a chance to reunite with former teachers and friends, creating lasting memories before venturing off to college.

Even after a separation of less than ten years, students often discover numerous changes upon returning to their former schools. Some are pleasantly surprised by the transformations, while others find that certain aspects have remained unchanged. Interestingly, even when encountering the same teachers, students' perceptions can vary significantly. Some remember these educators as the best they ever had, cherishing their guidance and influence, while others may not hold them in the same high regard.

As time progresses, it becomes apparent that students take different paths in life. Some of them have emerged as the respected valedictorians of their graduating class, excelling academically and achieving remarkable accomplishments. Conversely, there are those who barely graduated and are preparing to enter the workforce as skilled laborers.

However, even though Regina did not start her studying in grade school, she will remember her first United States English professor with a great deal of disappointment, and I must take responsibility for that.

Dr. Notsowisedog, as I will refer to him here, was an individual who initially exhibited prejudiced behavior and played a significant role in Regina's early journey. It is important to note that "Dr. Notsowisedog" is a pseudonym used to protect his identity. He served as Regina's first English instructor and had a lasting impact on her progress.

When Regina began her education in the United States, it became evident that her English skills needed improvement. Therefore, I suggested that she consider enrolling in ESL (English as a Second Language) classes offered by colleges. I specifically advised against suggesting low-level regular English classes, as those may have included native speakers who also struggled with English, potentially hindering her progress.

However, as time passed, it became evident that Regina's writing and reading abilities were already at a level suitable for regular college.

During this period in Regina's life, which took place before the birth of my first child, Lauren, Regina possessed a slender figure and radiated youthful beauty. While she continues to retain her beauty, it is important to note that her appearance is just one aspect of her overall persona. At the time, she was in her early twenties, embarking on her journey in the United States, filled with a sense of curiosity and adventure. I hope Regina understands the intention behind my previous sentences and doesn't take offense, as they were meant in a lighthearted manner.

Anyway, for most of her life, Regina had studied in Korea, and upon coming to the United States, she introduced new aspects of the American style of learning. She embraced concepts like interactive classroom environments, encouraging constant eye contact, and promoting the idea that it is acceptable to challenge professors if one feels they are incorrect. These approaches brought a fresh perspective to her learning experience, fostering an environment of active engagement and critical thinking.

Unlike myself, who had spent most of my life in the U.S. and had become accustomed to the aforementioned aspects of the American style of learning, Regina had a challenging time adjusting to them. These practices that came naturally to me were new and unfamiliar to her, requiring her to adapt and find her footing in this different educational environment.

When Regina took Dr. Notsowisedog's class, she faced significant struggles, but it was primarily due to his inadequate teaching. For instance, within the first two weeks of the class, Regina approached me and shared that Professor Notsowisedog had informed her that the class was not suitable for her due to her poor English skills. I questioned the reason behind his judgment, to which she explained that on the first day of class, he had instructed everyone to write a short essay about themselves on a piece of paper. Based solely on her writing, he concluded that her skills were insufficient to continue in the class.

I advised Regina to approach Dr. Notsowisedog and request a review of her writing, asking him to specify the areas in which he believed she needed improvement. Regina hesitated, believing that she could not question the professor's decision. I reassured her that in this country, we have the right to inquire about decisions and that it is a fundamental aspect of the learning process. Encouraged by this, she bravely scheduled a meeting with Dr. Notsowisedog to address her concerns.

Unfortunately, during their meeting, Dr. Notsowisedog mistakenly brought another Asian girl's paper and began critiquing it, assuming it was Regina's. Regina promptly corrected him, stating that the name on the paper was not hers. Dr. Notsowisedog then retrieved Regina's paper and casually remarked that it appeared fine before swiftly moving on, offering little in the way of an apology.

Despite considering dropping the class, Regina was resolute in not allowing her first American class to end in failure. She was determined to persevere and demonstrate her capabilities. Reluctantly, we made the decision to continue with the class; however, looking back, it proved to be an unfortunate mistake. As they say, always follow the duck theory: if something smells like a duck, looks like a duck, walks like a duck, and acts like a duck, then it's most likely a duck.

Regina consistently pointed out that throughout the semester, there was a noticeable difference in the way the instructor treated students from Eastern parts of Asia compared to those from the rest of the group, including South America, non-English speaking regions of the Western world, and Africa.

When one of Regina's main projects received an unexpectedly low grade, she expressed her desire to have another meeting with the instructor, this time with my support, to discuss his feedback. Upon examining the assignment, it seemed fairly decent considering her level. However, I couldn't help but express my disbelief that a specialized class for foreign students, like Regina, seemed to lack understanding of their needs, especially since the instructor frequently emphasized his extensive experience teaching the course for over 20 years and provided insights on what to expect. I was tempted to express my concerns, thinking that perhaps it was time for him to consider retiring because he seemed unsure of what he was doing.

In addition to the situation, Dr. Notsowisedog made a threatening gesture to record Regina's speech conversation, which constituted a part of her final exam. I nonchalantly suggested that recording the final was an excellent idea. Dr. Notsowisedog gave me an odd look and inquired why. I pointed out that he would likely be recording the speech conversation finals of all his students, right? This seemed to fluster him and provoke a slight anger. I reassured him that if any doubts arose about my wife's performance, I would appreciate the opportunity to compare it with the performance of his other students.

Boy, deep down, I secretly hoped that he would target my accents and confront me, just as he had done with many other students, by saying something like "I have trouble understanding you." However, to my surprise, he didn't fall into that trap.

Our meeting concluded with an awkward silence, but I am confident that my message resonated with him. Regina expressed her fear of returning to his class and completing what she had started. She repeatedly mentioned that in Korea, she would be marked with a metaphorical "scarlet letter A" from this point onward. In response, I assured Regina that this country would be different and that he would never be able to manipulate or mistreat her.

Two weeks before the scheduled speech conversation finals, I received a phone call from the dean of Dr. Notso-wisedog's college. She requested to speak with me regard-ing Regina's conversational final. The dean proposed the idea of having Regina's final conducted by her instead of Dr. Notsowisedog and asked if I was okay with it.

I didn't inquire about the reasons behind the dean's pro-posal, but I had a strong suspicion. The final consisted of three questions: "Are you an international student?", "What does your husband do?", and "Where does he work?".

To provide further clarification for those who may not fully grasp the significance of the questions, it is crucial to understand that passing the final exam was not mandatory for Regina's green card status. However, it held significant importance for international students due to the depart-ment's strong influence over their student visa standing. This means that throughout all these years, there were no students present to question the incompetence of the professor and seek guidance on what to do. It seems that he was running his class with an authoritarian approach, acting as if he were the sole authority.

The questions aimed to determine Regina's status as an international student, even though she already held a green card, indicating her permanent residency in the United States. It's important to note that this specific course was not a mandatory requirement for her residency, and no green card holder had taken this class prior to Regina.

It's difficult to believe that those were the actual questions presented by the dean of the school during the final examination. I really wish it were a fabricated tale.

Chapter 17

Yes, I'm very proud of you and your college choice.

From: Lauren To
To: santa claws

Dearsanta Glaus, I know
I did a lot of bad things. I
also know I did a lot of
great and good things. I am
very very very very very
very very very very
sorry for the bad things
I did. I hope you can understand. I promise I will
make it up. And after
I do can you plese give
me my gifts. I'want toys:
Like a barbie house with
the fernicher and the food
and the other stuff, also can
I have all the Lego friends
even the new ones, can I
also have a Phone iPad and
computer, and a new big
bike with training wheels
and Last but not least
to wish you a marry
chrirstmis!!!
        Marry chrirstmis
                    Love Lauren

When my kids were little, and they are still little to me,
I used to tell them this story. As Daddy was growing up, we
didn't have much. Whenever I asked my mom and dad to
buy something, it never happened. While my friends got to
play Nintendo and other game consoles, I didn't even know
those consoles existed. When I found out that everyone
knew about them, it made me feel sad. I secretly wished

that my dad wasn't my real dad. I imagined that one day, my real rich dad, like the CEO of Samsung, would knock on my door and tell me that I'm his long-lost son. It was like a scene from a movie.

But that day never came, and as I grew older, I realized I looked exactly like my dad. There was no hope of a sudden change in fortune, ha-ha. You see, your dad dreamed of driving a Mercedes, but he could only afford a Hyundai. Your mom longed for steak dinners, but we always ended up going to Burger King with coupons instead.

That's just how life is sometimes. You can't always get what you want, but you make the best of what you have. And yes, I want to assure you all that none of you are adopted, and there's no chance of new biological parents showing up. Our family is what we have, and we should cherish and appreciate it. We may not have all the luxuries, but we have love, support, and each other, which are far more valuable than material possessions.

The kids have heard that story many times, so they understand that life isn't always fair. They've learned that things don't always go as planned, and sometimes we face challenges and disappointments. However, they also know the importance of resilience and making the best of every situation.

My oldest kid, Lauren, is about to go to college in a few months. I wanted to take this opportunity to share Lauren's incredible accomplishments with all of you. Throughout her high school years, Lauren attended a Blue Ribbon High School and achieved impressive academic results. She obtained a remarkable SAT score of 1490 and an ACT score of 34, truly showcasing her dedication and intelligence. With a GPA of 4.5 (where a typical 4.0 is considered an A), she has rightfully earned the position of class valedictorian.

What sets Lauren apart is her drive for excellence and her commitment to continuous learning. In addition to her high school diploma, Lauren is expected to receive her associate degree in science, an extraordinary feat that demonstrates her exceptional academic abilities and ambition.

Lauren excelled in all her AP classes, earning a perfect score of 5 in most of them, with the exception of English where she received a score of 4. Her passion for education extends beyond her own success. She took the initiative to establish a free tutoring program that has positively impacted over 200 students from more than 15 schools within the district. With over 30 dedicated tutors involved, this program has become a valuable resource for academic support.

Beyond excelling in academics, Lauren has exhibited re-markable leadership skills and a deep dedication to making a positive impact in her community. Her outstanding efforts were recognized when she received the highly esteemed Youth Advocate of the Year Award from a national organi-zation focused on tobacco-free campaigns. This prestigious award acknowledged Lauren's significant contributions in promoting a healthier environment in Washington D.C. The event was graced by esteemed guests, including Nancy Pelosi, who joined in honoring Lauren's accomplishments.

Lauren's artistic talents are equally impressive. At the age of 14, she achieved the remarkable accomplishment of writing and publishing her own book titled "Am I Allowed to Be a Kid?", a testament to her exceptional writing skills and creativity. Additionally, she showcased her poetic talents by achieving 3rd place in a state-level poetry competition called Poetry Out Loud.

Lauren's achievements have not gone unnoticed, as she has received accolades and recognition from various sources. She was honored with the State Governor's High Achievement Award and received commendations from city mayors, school principals, and the superintendent.

These accomplishments are a reflection of Lauren's exceptional academic performance, leadership abilities, community involvement, and artistic talents. I couldn't be prouder of her, and I'm confident that she will continue to make a positive impact in college and beyond.

It's important to acknowledge her accomplishments. However, it is with mixed emotions that I share the news that despite her impressive track record, Lauren faced rejection from every single school she applied to, including prestigious Ivy League institutions, Chicago, Rice, Stanford, and UC colleges, with the exception of local state colleges.

What bothers us the most is that a few of Lauren's classmates were accepted into those prestigious schools despite having achievements that fall far below Lauren's. It can be frustrating to witness such discrepancies.

I guess it's too late to change Asian to Non-Asian minority box now.

I understand that college admissions can be an incredibly competitive and challenging process, and it can be difficult to accept if your own child faces rejection from their desired schools. It's natural to feel disappointed and frustrated when things don't turn out as expected, especially when you know your child is qualified and deserving of a spot.

Fortunately, both Lauren and our family have success-fully moved beyond the initial sadness and have embraced the next chapter with optimism. This transition was rela-tively smooth, as I have consistently made efforts to teach my children about the realities of life's fairness from an early age. They have learned that life doesn't always go as planned, and we may not always get what we want. However, we have also learned the importance of making the best of what we have and finding joy in the present moment. This perspective has helped us navigate through disappointments and appreciate the blessings in our lives. We have embraced the understanding that while we can't always control the circumstances, we have the power to choose how we respond and make the most out of every sit-uation. It's a valuable lesson that will continue to guide us as we face new opportunities and challenges in the future.

I wanted to tell my daughter, Lauren, how deeply I love her and how incredibly proud I am of all her achievements. When you received that last rejection letter from the schools you applied to and tears welled up in your eyes, it shattered my heart to witness your disappointment. It was an immense challenge for me to conceal my own emotions during that moment.

I want you to know that I saw the effort and dedication you put into your applications, and I believed in you every step of the way. Seeing you in tears and hearing you say that you had tried your best made it even harder to witness. But please remember, my dear, that this moment does not define you or your future.

I have no doubt that your time will come, and when it does, you will have the biggest smile on your face. Your journey may have taken an unexpected turn, but I want you to know that I will be by your side through it all. You are resilient, talented, and full of potential.

Never forget that my love for you is unwavering, and my pride in you goes far beyond any college acceptance letter. Your worth and abilities extend far beyond the decisions of a few institutions. You have already achieved so much, and I have no doubt that you will continue to achieve greatness in whatever path you choose.

I believe in you, Lauren, and I will always be your biggest cheerleader. Remember, setbacks and rejections are just stepping stones on the road to success. Your determination, passion, and perseverance will lead you to a future that is bright and fulfilling.

I love you more than words can express, and I am honored to be your parent.

Chapter 18

Three

I would like to tell my kids about their daddy's academic achievements and success in his studies. However, I must be honest with you. It was actually mommy, Regina, who graduated from college with honors and maintained an outstanding GPA. Although she faced some challenges in nursing school, she persevered and excelled. Mommy also passed her NCLEX exam on her first attempt and effortlessly obtained multiple certifications. She was an exceptional student, and I am immensely proud of her accomplishments.

In fact, Daddy's college experience was not on par with Mommy's. I distinctly recall enrolling in a mandatory 400-level statistics course taught by a Russian professor, and it proved to be quite demanding for me. Right from the outset, I sensed trouble looming over me during the first week of the class.

The professor collected our first homework assignments that morning and made a comment. He said, "I see that everyone has handed in their first homework assignment today. Some of you handed it in with your name face up, while others handed it in blank side up. Since we have 18 students here, and the person who handed it in follows the person in front of them, only 75% of the time, what is the probability that the last person's name is face up if the first person handed it in face up?". And those 15 minutes the professor gave us to complete the assignment were not enough for me. To be honest, even if he had given me the whole day, I would have still struggled. The material was challenging, and I found it difficult to grasp. It was definitely a tough experience for me in that statistics class.

When we had our first exam, and I received my test result, it was a disappointing '3'. No, it wasn't a score of 30; it was simply three out of 100. I had experienced some poor test scores before, but this was by far the lowest. It felt disheartening, and I knew an 'F' grade was likely looming over me. However, dropping the class or withdrawing from the semester wasn't an option due to the university's strict policy of allowing only 12 credits of dropped classes.

Despite the setback, I had to continue with the course. Fortunately, in the following semester, I had a different professor teaching the class. With renewed determination and hard work, I was able to pass the class. It was a relief to overcome the challenges and see improvement in my academic performance. It taught me the importance of resilience and perseverance in the face of difficulties.

I have already shared this story with Lauren, Andrew, and Kristen several times, but it's worth repeating. It's perfectly normal to have some bad marks from time to time. Just look at your daddy's journey—despite facing challenges and setbacks in college, I have managed to do pretty well now, haven't I? It's important to remember that a few poor grades do not define your capabilities or determine your future success. What truly matters is how you learn from those experiences, persevere, and continue working hard towards your goals.

By recounting my own experiences of encountering challenges and setbacks, I have provided them with a grounded perspective. They grasp the notion that scores of 50% or 60% should not cause distress or tears, as your dad has set a relatively low benchmark. I stress the significance of learning from mistakes, persisting in the face of adversity, and aiming for progress. I want them to understand that their value is not defined by grades alone but by their tenacity and ability to bounce back. My aim is to cultivate a positive mindset and foster belief in their capacity to overcome obstacles, much like I did.

Chapter 19

Goal Setting

During the COVID-19 pandemic, parents faced numerous challenges. With schools closed, we had to bring our children home, which added to the financial strain we were already experiencing. The increased cost of living and rising food prices further impacted our wallets, making it even more difficult to make ends meet.

I wish I could say that I had foreseen the challenges ahead and prepared accordingly. However, the truth is that it was simply a stroke of luck that I had purchased a house and car before the pandemic hit. It provided some stability during these uncertain times.

As supplies became scarce, even something as simple as toilet paper became a valuable commodity. I was fortunate enough to secure a few rolls before the scarcity reached its peak, ensuring we had enough for our family.

With all three kids at home full-time, I had to establish some structure and guidance to help them navigate this new normal. One of the first things I realized was the importance of setting clear goals for each of my children.

Lauren, as the oldest, had a clear sense of what she wanted to achieve, but Andrew and Kristen were struggling to find their own paths.

I worked closely with them, helping them explore their interests, strengths, and aspirations. We had numerous conversations, discussing their passions and potential career paths. It was essential for them to understand that finding their own goals takes time and self-discovery.

Kristen's goal was relatively straightforward. I printed out daily and weekly worksheets for her to practice math skills, and we had plenty of chapter books available for her to read. She had a routine in place that helped her stay engaged and focused on her learning.

However, Andrew faced a more significant challenge in finding his own goal. He occasionally felt that he was being treated unfairly in comparison to his older sister, Lauren. He perceived that I spent more time with her than with him.

I understand Andrew's concerns and acknowledge that balancing attention between siblings can be difficult at times. While it may have seemed like I spent more time with Lauren due to her specific goals and needs, it was never my intention to make Andrew feel neglected or less important.

I encouraged Andrew to explore his own passions and talents, but it wasn't easy for him to find something that truly sparked his interest. We had discussions about various hobbies and activities, but nothing seemed to resonate with him.

One day, while I was watching a YouTuber talk about the future of AI and the importance of human coding, an idea struck me. I thought about teaching coding to Andrew, even though I didn't have a deep understanding of it myself. I remembered my own struggles with computer programming back in college, finding it boring and challenging. Nonetheless, I mentioned it to Andrew, thinking it might be worth exploring.

To my surprise, Andrew's reaction was anything but what I expected. He took an interest in coding, and with the help of online tutorials and resources, he began teaching himself C++. He would spend hours watching seemingly boring and complex coding lessons on YouTube, pausing and replaying them until he fully grasped the concepts.

Over the course of the last two months, Andrew's dedication and determination paid off. He mastered the C++ programming language all on his own. His progress was astounding, and I couldn't have been prouder.

It became evident that Andrew's goal in learning coding went beyond impressing his dad or gaining more attention than his sister, Lauren. Through this journey, he found his own passion and developed a strong sense of self-confidence and fulfillment. Coding became a means of self-expression and a pathway to explore his creativity.

Witnessing Andrew's transformation has been truly remarkable. It taught me the importance of supporting my children in finding their own unique paths, even if it takes them outside of my comfort zone. I have learned that their journey of self-discovery can lead to incredible achievements and personal growth.

I am excited to see where Andrew's coding skills take him in the future. Most importantly, I am grateful for the lessons he has taught me about embracing new challenges and encouraging my children to pursue their passions, even if they seem daunting at first.

Parenting multiple children can be a delicate balancing act, but I am dedicated to fostering a nurturing environment where both of my children feel valued and supported.

By that time, my friend and mentor Billy mentioned to me that Andrew should sign up for the Congressional App Development Contest. Billy thought it would be a great opportunity for Andrew to showcase his coding skills and creativity. Intrigued by the idea, I shared the contest details with Andrew, and he became excited about the prospect of participating.

With his newfound passion for coding, Andrew eagerly started working on his app development project. We brainstormed ideas and diligently researched different concepts to create a unique and impactful application. Andrew was determined to demonstrate his skills and make a lasting impression. As the deadline for the contest approached, Andrew completed his app and submitted it for consideration. The sense of accomplishment and pride he felt was immeasurable.

The following year, Andrew's dedication and hard work paid off as he was named the winner of the Congressional App contest for our congressional district. His achievement was celebrated, and the local newspaper featured his photograph on the very front page, recognizing his remarkable accomplishment.

What made Andrew's victory even more impressive was the fact that he surpassed competitors from high school programs, despite being a middle school programmer. His talent, determination, and innovative app set him apart from the rest, making him the national winner of the Congressional App contest.

Winning this prestigious competition brought well-deserved recognition for Andrew and opened doors to new opportunities. The experience provided him with invaluable learning experiences, allowing him to further develop his skills, expand his knowledge, and explore his passion for app development.

As a parent, I couldn't be prouder of Andrew for taking the initiative to participate in such a prestigious competition. His journey from self-learning coding through YouTube tutorials to actively pursuing a national app development contest is a testament to his resilience, talent, and determination.

This achievement showcases Andrew's ability to excel in a highly competitive field and highlights his potential for future success. I am excited to continue supporting him as he nurtures his passion for coding and app development, and I can't wait to see the incredible things he will accomplish in the years to come.

Chapter 20

Billy's Wishlist

If you are a regular churchgoer, you may be familiar with the Parable of the Ten Virgins. It is a well-known story in Christian teachings.

In the story, ten bridesmaids or virgins are waiting for the arrival of the bridegroom. Five of them are described as wise because they bring extra oil for their lamps, while the other five are considered foolish because they did not bring any extra oil. As they wait, the bridegroom is delayed, and all ten virgins fall asleep. When the cry is made that the bridegroom is approaching, the virgins wake up and prepare their lamps. However, the five foolish virgins realize that their lamps are running out of oil, so they ask the wise virgins for some oil. The wise virgins refuse, fearing that there may not be enough for all of them. The foolish virgins then go to buy more oil, but while they are away, the bridegroom arrives, and the wise virgins enter the wedding feast with him. When the foolish virgins return, they find the door locked and are not allowed in.

I heard this story many times since I was a child. I always connecting the Parable of the Ten Virgins often associated with being watchful for God's arrival, it can also remind us to be prepared and proactive in our everyday lives.

My friend Billy's decision to voluntarily step down from a high management position to pursue an engineering career is unique and inspiring. While such bold career changes may be uncommon in my workplace, I appreciate his dedication to following his passion. Initially, I had some doubts about his leadership capabilities, but after working with him closely for a few months, those doubts vanished. He proved to be sharp and capable in his new role.

And he had a clear sense of what he wanted to achieve in life.

But despite his decision to step down from a management position, he still expressed a willingness to support me in my career aspirations if I genuinely desired to pursue that path.

Returning to Billy's story, upon receiving the official word, Billy's boss instructed him to create a comprehensive "wish list" of the specific needs and desires of his department. This process entailed gathering input from all personnel and identifying desired items, including new equipment, software, furniture, and training opportunities. The wish list required detailed information, including barcodes, funding amounts, and explanations for each item, providing a comprehensive understanding of why each request was necessary.

Billy was informed that there might come a day when someone higher up would ask for the wish list, and if he and his department were not prepared, the funding could be bypassed to someone who was ready with their requests.

The timeline for such requests was usually very short, and if they heard the news late, it would be too late to respond effectively. It was essential to be proactive and have the wish list ready to seize funding opportunities when they arose.

If we're not adequately prepared, we may miss out on the opportunity to be rewarded. Being ready and proactive allows us to seize opportunities and increase our chances of receiving rewards or benefits. Preparedness and readiness play a significant role in maximizing our potential for success and recognition.

Do you create your wish list annually?

Chapter 21

11PM @ Walmart

One of the things that the Covid-19 pandemic took away from us was the opportunity to enjoy 24-hour shopping at Walmart. Regina and I used to cherish those late evening shopping trips where we could browse and take our time without any interruptions. It was a peaceful and relaxing experience, with few or no other shoppers around.

Unfortunately, due to the pandemic, Walmart had to adjust its operating hours and implement safety measures to protect customers and staff. The 24-hour shopping option was temporarily suspended, and we had to adapt to new shopping routines and limited hours.

Well, I once shared a hypothetical scenario with Lauren and Andrew. Imagine you and I were shopping in Walmart around 11pm, and suddenly we find ourselves standing in front of none other than Bill Gates. He's browsing the aisles, looking for something, and we strike up a conversation. As the conversation unfolds, he asks you the question, "It's your lucky day! What can I do for you in return?"

Now, this hypothetical question is meant to make us reflect on our dreams and aspirations. It encourages us to think about what we truly desire and what impact we want to make in our lives and the world around us.

So, are you ready for that question? Take a moment to consider what you would ask for if you had such a remarkable opportunity. It's a chance to think big and envision how you could create positive change or fulfill a personal goal.

Andrew and Lauren were initially stumped by the question, unable to provide an immediate answer. However, it was a thought-provoking moment that sparked something within Lauren. Inspired by the conversation, she found her creative voice and embarked on a journey to write a book.

With determination and passion, Lauren poured her thoughts and ideas onto the pages, weaving a captivating story that reflected her unique perspective. Despite facing challenges along the way, she persisted and ultimately completed her book. Publishing her book was a significant achievement for Lauren. It allowed her to share her thoughts, emotions, and imagination with a wider audience. Through her writing, she discovered the power of storytelling and the impact it could have on others.

Lauren, I am writing this book now because you have inspired me with your determination and accomplishments. You have shown incredible dedication in pursuing your passions and achieving your goals. I want to acknowledge that I have not always been a perfect role model, and I recognize the importance of leading by example.

As a parent, it is my responsibility to guide and support you, but I also understand that actions speak louder than words. I have realized that it is essential for me to not only give you advice but also demonstrate through my own actions the values and principles that I believe in.

Chapter 22

Types of Punishments

I heard about another school shooting that occurred this year. It's disheartening to see that school shootings have become more common and expected in some areas and schools. However, it's important to remember that school shootings are still relatively rare occurrences in most educational settings.

It's true that when tragic events like school shootings occur, there tends to be a range of opinions on what factors may have contributed to them. People often express various viewpoints, including blaming violent video games, inadequate gun control measures, or shortcomings in school teachers and administrators.

I believe that a nurturing and supportive home environment plays a crucial role in a child's development, including their mental and emotional well-being. Positive parenting, open communication, and providing a stable and loving home can have a significant impact on a child's overall

behavior and attitude toward violence. However, it's important to approach this complex issue with a comprehensive
understanding. School shootings are the result of a multi-
tude of factors, and no single factor can be solely attributed
as the cause. It's crucial to consider a combination of societal, psychological, and systemic factors that contribute to
these incidents.

I attended a large high school on the East Coast. Our
graduating class comprised nearly 700 students, and we had
over 1,200 incoming freshmen. While fights after school
were a regular occurrence, it was important to note that
weapons were never used. In our high school, there was a
consensus that using weapons was not cool or acceptable.
Interestingly, something amusing would happen after a few
weeks: the individuals who had been involved in the fist
fights would often become good friends.

It's important to note that physical altercations are generally not encouraged or condoned as a way to address conflicts. But physical conflicts can and do sometimes occur
among young boys, and there may be instances where they
choose to "duke it out" as a means of resolving their differences.

When I received a phone call from Andrew's principal,
I was taken aback to learn that my son was involved in
a fistfight with his long-time friend, Mal. It came as a
surprise because Mal and Andrew had known each other
since childhood and even played soccer together on the
same team for multiple seasons. I immediately recognized
that my son Andrew was entering the stage of adolescence,
where he would undoubtedly encounter various challenges
and learn valuable life lessons. Understanding the situation,
I made sure to express my deep disappointment to Andrew

and stressed the significance of apologizing to Mal for his actions. However, before we had a chance to address the issue, Mal 's mom reached out to me and offered her apologies first. Although I missed the opportunity to address the situation myself, I felt relieved that despite the incident, our friendship remained intact. We were able to move past it and continue being good friends.

Ultimately, both Andrew and Mal were able to reconcile and restore their friendship. The incident served as a valuable lesson for Andrew, and he will likely remember the impact of his actions for a long time. Overall, things have improved significantly, and I'm grateful that they were able to mend their friendship.

By the way, that was the one and only time my son Andrew has been involved in any physical altercation with anyone so far.

A few years ago, I came across a news story that highlighted a football player who faced consequences for using corporal punishment on his own child as a form of discipline. The incident resulted in disciplinary action from the NFL, reflecting the organization's stance against such behavior.

This incident raised important discussions about the appropriate methods of disciplining children and the potential consequences of using corporal punishment. It served as a reminder that as parents, we have a responsibility to ensure the well-being and safety of our children while also promoting positive and respectful forms of discipline.

During a conversation with an older co-worker, they shared their personal experience of corporal punishment that was common during their time in school. They recounted how there was a prominent disciplinary tool: a large paddle kept in the principal's office. They mentioned that, occasionally, misbehaving boys would face physical discipline in the form of a "smack" with the paddle.

It's important to recognize that disciplinary practices have indeed evolved over time, reflecting the advancement of societal norms and our understanding of child development. While corporal punishment may have been more accepted in the past, there is growing consensus among educational institutions and experts that non-violent and positive disciplinary approaches are generally more beneficial. However, whether these approaches are better or worse depends on various factors and individual perspectives.

I hold the belief that corporal punishment should only be applied up until the middle school level, and even then, it should be approached with extreme caution to ensure it does not cross the line into abuse. It is crucial to distinguish between appropriate discipline and actions that leave visible marks or cause lasting harm. Personally, I consider any form of punishment that leaves physical marks or injuries beyond the immediate disciplinary purpose to be abusive.

Andrew told me that during the pandemic, he and his friend often have conversations about the various types of discipline they receive at home when they misbehave. According to Andrew, he observed that different families may employ varying disciplinary methods. For instance, he mentioned that in African American households, the use of a belt as a form of discipline is more commonly seen. In families with Asian backgrounds, the use of sticks may be employed, whereas in Hispanic households, it is not uncommon for parents to use shoes or any nearby kitchen object for disciplinary purposes. Interestingly, Andrew and his friends were surprised to discover that white families tend to rely less on physical discipline and instead utilize methods such as time-outs. It is important to note that these observations are generalizations and may not apply to every family within each cultural background. These are the exact words conveyed by my son, so please refrain from any unwarranted criticism.

Andrew mentioned that he personally finds the absence of physical discipline in white households a stark contrast. His friend, coming from a white family, had even expressed his determination to contact the authorities by dialing 911 if he ever witnessed any physical discipline taking place.

All the kids, including Andrew, found it amusing when they discussed the idea of threatening their parents by calling for help. However, their laughter stemmed from the fact that minority parents had a unique way of handling such threats. Instead of being scared, their parents would playfully respond by saying, "If you call for help, we'll send you to the foster family for good!" It was a lighthearted way of letting the children know that their parents were not to be intimidated and that their love and discipline came from a place of care.

Andrew shared an interesting incident where a white kid decided to report to the school personnel about potential physical abuse at home. As a result, the school authorities intervened and spoke to all the children, inquiring if they experienced any form of physical abuse in their households. This incident had a significant impact, and after that, no more white kids could join the discussions about home discipline that the minority kids had. It appears that the incident has created an atmosphere of caution, causing the white children to feel excluded from such conversations, even if some minority children vouch for their inclusion.

I believe that children understand the reasons behind receiving corporal punishment from their parents. With the exception of a few outliers, most parents strive to guide their children in the right direction. Some argue that a few well-deserved spankings from parents can serve as a deterrent, potentially preventing children from engaging in behaviors that could lead to more severe consequences, such as criminal activities.

However, it is important to note that the effectiveness of corporal punishment as a deterrent or a preventive measure is a matter of debate. Many experts and organizations caution against its use, advocating for alternative disciplinary approaches that prioritize positive reinforcement, open communication, and teaching appropriate behaviors. But I must say, those experts are nowhere to be found when these kids grow up and become career criminals.

Additionally, it is worth noting that the effectiveness of any disciplinary method varies from individual to individual. What works for one person may not work for another due to their unique circumstances, personalities, and experiences.

I have noticed this pattern with my three children. The girls quickly moved on and learned from their mistakes, behaving differently in similar situations. However, Andrew seems to have a harder time focusing on the underlying issues that led to the punishment, instead focusing on the temporary pain he experienced as a result of the spanking.

My eldest, Lauren, once recounted an incident when she, Andrew, and Kristen spent a few nights at my brother's house in Boston. During their stay, their Caucasian Aunt Tracy, who was born and raised in Alabama, utilized a time-out method to address their cousin Michael's misbehavior towards them. It proved to be incredibly effective, as Michael developed a fear of being alone in his room as a consequence of the time-outs.

Curious about whether this method would work in our family, I asked Lauren for her opinion. After pondering for a few seconds, she responded that it would probably not work for our family, but she believed that Andrew would enjoy it.

Finally, I want to underscore the importance of completely banning corporal punishment for parents who struggle to control their anger. It can be likened to a harmful addiction, where the urge to release your anger through physical punishment can lead to increasingly severe actions against your child. The ease with which self-control can be lost highlights the danger of using corporal punishment as a means to appease yourself rather than genuinely aiding your child's development. I strongly urge that if you find yourself fitting into this category, it's crucial to support the complete ban of corporal punishment. Your commitment to this cause can make a significant difference in ensuring the well-being of children.

Chapter 23

Ryan

I have a sister-in-law named Jennifer who currently lives in Canada. She is one of Regina's younger sisters but got married before her. In the States, it's not really a big deal, but in Korea, it used to be considered a significant matter.

Initially, Regina wasn't even invited to Jennifer's wedding because she was the older sibling but hadn't gotten married yet. This decision was strongly recommended by their grandparents to follow the traditional norms. However, Regina and Jennifer went against this recommended tradition and decided to enjoy Jennifer's wedding day together.

Jennifer got married in her early 20s and didn't have a child until Lauren and Andrew came along. Jennifer was overjoyed when she found out she was having a boy. Ryan, their son, is incredibly adorable and bears a strong resemblance to his mother, with an added touch of handsomeness.

When Jennifer wanted to visit her sister Regina in the States with her son, we were thrilled about the stay and looked forward to it. However, our excitement was accompanied by a little shock. It became evident that Ryan, the boy, seemed quite spoiled and didn't behave like my own children.

For instance, when I would announce that it was time to eat, my kids would eagerly gather around the table, assist their mom in setting the table with chopsticks and spoons, and patiently wait for the meal. They understood the importance of not wasting food and that they needed to finish what was served, or else they wouldn't get anything else. However, I noticed that Jennifer had to constantly beg Ryan to sit still and spoon-feed him every other bite. Additionally, I discovered that the 5-year-old was not fully potty trained and frequently threw tantrums.

Worst of all, Jennifer appeared to enable her son's behavior and allowed him to persist in his disruptive actions. Although she expressed sympathy towards us regarding his behavior, she made it clear that Ryan would be her only child, and she wanted to indulge him until he matured a bit more. I was taken aback and puzzled by her approach, but I recognized that it wasn't my place to enforce my parenting views upon them. Moreover, I reminded myself that their stay with us was only for a week, so it would be a temporary situation.

A few years later, our entire extended family gathered in Canada for a family gathering. I was pleasantly surprised by the significant growth I witnessed in Ryan, both physically and emotionally. He had transformed into a perfectly bilingual child who displayed utmost respect and embraced both modern and traditional values. It was truly impressive to see the positive change since the last time I met him. This experience taught me a valuable lesson: the approach of "one size fits all" does not apply to everyone. I had always believed that being somewhat strict with your own children was the best way to raise them, but observing Ryan's development served as a reminder that different approaches can yield positive results. It was another valuable lesson learned from a close relative, and it made me appreciate the joys of witnessing a child's growth and development.

Chapter 24

Dr. Georgopoulos

Dr. Georgopoulos, a highly esteemed physics professor, is widely recognized for his exceptional teaching abilities and numerous accolades as a multiple-time recipient of the Best Teaching Award. Nearly thirty years ago, I had the privilege of being a student in his class. While it is true that his teaching style was characterized by strictness and lacked overt supportiveness, I firmly believe that it ultimately proved effective in nurturing intellectual growth. Dr. Georgopoulos possessed an argumentative nature and fearlessly challenged his students, recognizing that this approach would enhance their learning experience. His willingness to provide constructive criticism, even if it momentarily caused offense, originated from a genuine belief that it would ultimately benefit his students.

During one instance, when Dr. Georgopoulos was discussing the concept of a free body diagram, he used arrows to depict different forces, like the downward arrow indicating weight, the upward arrow representing the normal force, arrows indicating various friction forces in different directions, and arrows representing forces. He employed different arrow orientations to signify the magnitudes and directions of different forces, effectively conveying the principles involved. Then He remarked, "You see all these arrows pointing everywhere, but you won't find no Indians today." I am confident that such remarks will not be acceptable in 2023, but it is important to remember that those remarks were reflective of his character at that time.

The effectiveness of this approach may be a topic open to debate, as different students have varying experiences. Those who struggled in his class often question his teaching abilities, asserting that he falls short of being a good instructor.

He viewed his class as a means to identify those who were not well-suited for engineering, serving as a challenging crucible for aspiring engineers. And he was proven right. We had to relocate the class twice to smaller classrooms before reaching the final, as a result of numerous students dropping out.

It was akin to a Navy SEAL's hell week, but if you can survive, you will be forever recognized as a SEAL.

In my personal opinion, however, I consider Dr. Georgopoulos to be the best teacher I have ever encountered. His unwavering approach compelled me to push my limits and broaden my understanding of physics. Although he often called me out and pointed out my mistakes, using the phrase "No guacamole for you!", I believe his intention was to challenge and motivate me. While it is true that his methods did not resonate with everyone, there was one incident that stands out when he unintentionally made a girl in our class cry by questioning, "I asked you how old are you? but you keep telling me you're 25 cents." Nonetheless,

I maintain the belief that his strict and demanding approach effectively distinguished those who were sincerely dedicated to the subject and willing to devote the required effort to achieve success.

Chapter 25

Mr. Cho

When I was accepted into graduate school for mathematics, the experience was markedly different from my time as an undergraduate student. One notable change was the assignment of my own small office, providing me with a dedicated space to work and study. This felt like a significant milestone in my academic journey, signifying a higher level of independence and responsibility.

Moreover, as a graduate assistant, I had the valuable opportunity to serve as an instructor for a remedial class. Taking on this role allowed me to acquire essential teaching experience while assisting students who were struggling with mathematical concepts. Guiding and supporting others in their learning journeys proved to be an immensely gratifying experience, enhancing my academic life in profound ways.

One unique aspect of the math department is that graduate assistants have the opportunity to teach their own classes, a privilege not typically offered in other departments. This distinction sets the math department apart and provides graduate students with invaluable teaching experience that complements their academic pursuits. Unlike other departments where teaching responsibilities are usually assigned to faculty members, the math department recognizes the importance of hands-on teaching experience for its graduate students. Also, there are numerous lower-level math courses that faculty members simply cannot handle, and this applies to most universities.

Overall, the transition from undergraduate to graduate school brought about exciting transformations, including the privilege of having my own office and the chance to instruct a remedial class. These experiences not only enriched my educational journey but also played a pivotal role in shaping me into a more well-rounded mathematician.

While I had not yet attained the status of a full professor like Dr. Georgopoulos, I aspired to become an effective and approachable educator, inspired by his exemplary teaching methods. My goal was to adopt a gentler approach, mirroring his style, and creating an engaging and inclusive learning environment for my students.

I typically initiate my classes by asking a simple question: "What is your favorite TV show?" For me, personally, I find enjoyment in watching "Married with Children." I assume many of you have come across this show at least once or twice. At the start of each semester, I always introduce the concept of the Bundy family philosophy to my students. It revolves around the notion that 'The Bundy family never loses because they never try.' This lighthearted remark is intended to convey the message that nobody in our class should give up, unless we happen to have a Mr. Bundy among us. This type of humor helps foster a friendly and approachable atmosphere in the classroom. As their instructor, I consider it my duty to ignite students' interest in learning and motivate them to unlock their full potential.

Thanks to Mr. Cho, I now have even more stories to share with my students. Similar to me, Mr. Cho was a graduate math student, but he held the esteemed position of being a Ph.D. candidate. This allowed him to teach higher-level math courses, although he often struggled with pronouncing the sound "p" as "f." You should definitely hear his entertaining hockey game story involving the phrase "hockey pucks." It's equally amusing to hear the experiences of another Cameroon graduate student who encounters difficulty pronouncing the sound "th" as "d." He humorously shares a story of referring to himself as being "30" while his wife was "30 too." In another lighthearted anecdote, Vietnamese students visit an agriculture department farm site and unintentionally ask about " free bull shits" instead of an open to public cow manure for their backyard garden.

In any case, our math graduate department was filled with entertainment. I was among the few Americans who shared office and study nights with individuals from diverse backgrounds. The pay as a graduate assistant was sufficient for me to live easily, but I witnessed my friends supporting their families with the meager income, and some even sent money back home.

I always made sure to have my office stocked with free coffee, chips, and crackers, and I never locked my door so that any of my international friends could freely grab and enjoy them. Additionally, I extended my assistance to them in accomplishing various tasks, such as helping them purchase a used car, register for insurance, or give rides to the local Wal-Marts. While high-level math posed its challenges,

I was fortunate to have plenty of the support and help of my close friends throughout my academic journey.

One day, Mr. Cho burst into my office with an excited expression on his face and exclaimed, "Andrew, you won't believe what just happened to me!" Curious, I inquired, "What happened?"

The story unfolds two weeks ago when Mr. Cho was in the midst of teaching his statistics class. To his surprise, one of his students abruptly walked out in the middle of the lecture. Recognizing that this had become a recurring behavior from the student in recent classes, Mr. Cho decided to devise a plan. He devised a simple, yet effective, pop quiz as a means to address the student's misconduct and impose a fitting consequence.

As Mr. Cho settled down to grade the stack of pop quiz papers, he noticed one particular paper that caught his attention—it was the very same paper submitted by the student who had left the class unexpectedly. Surprised by the sudden reappearance of the student's work, Mr. Cho's curiosity grew, and he eagerly began to examine the answers on the paper.

Taken aback by the unexpected turn of events, Mr. Cho couldn't help but wonder what had transpired. He carefully examined the handwriting on the paper, only to realize that it did not match his own. Realizing that someone had cheated on the previous test, he made a decision to address the issue with his entire class.

With a stern yet determined expression, Mr. Cho addressed the entire class, making it clear that he was fully aware of the cheating incident. He emphasized the seriousness of academic integrity and the consequences that could follow such misconduct. Mr. Cho provided the students with a one-week deadline to come forward and discuss the matter with him privately or else he would report the incident to the school dean's office.

To Mr. Cho's astonishment, more than half of the students in the class showed up to discuss what had transpired. They appeared genuinely concerned and willing to take responsibility for their actions. Curiously, I asked Mr. Cho what he was doing while they were taking the test. He replied, "Nothing, just reading a book."

However, to Mr. Cho's disappointment, the student he suspected of cheating never showed up during the designated period to discuss the incident. When confronted about the accusation, the student adamantly denied any wrongdoing. It was then revealed that the student's girlfriend, who was also in the same class, had written his name on the pop quiz paper instead of her own. She believed that he needed the extra points more than she did.

Mr. Cho presented the evidence and shared the details with the school dean's office. However, due to limitations in the available evidence, the dean's office could only take action against the girlfriend for her involvement in the incident. The students in the class began blaming everything on her, creating a tense and divisive atmosphere among the classmates. Mr. Cho gave the girl a stern warning and Mr. Cho wanted to make sure the girl understood the gravity of the situation and the potential damage it could cause to her reputation and academic record. Mr. Cho stressed the importance of taking responsibility for one's actions and learning from mistakes. Mr. Cho wanted the girl to understand the significance of owning up to her choices and the valuable lessons to be learned from them.

Chapter 26

Everybody Gets a Trophy

I have a long-time friend named Deb. Originally from South Dakota; she has been living in the same state as me for a considerable time. It seems like her family must have had access to some incredible water back in South Dakota because they all appear ageless. Despite knowing each other for such a long time, Deb never really expressed her preferences when it came to food. It wasn't until almost 20 years later that I discovered her aversion to fish and anything with a fishy flavor. During a Korean cooking class, I hosted at home, I finally discovered that Deb couldn't handle any food with a fish flavor. It was through her newlywed husband, John, that I learned about this preference of hers.

Over the many years of getting together for lunch and dinner occasions, Deb never mentioned her dislike for fish or fish-flavored foods. Perhaps she preferred to be accommodating and didn't want to hurt my feelings. However, it's crucial to remember that no one can read another person's mind unless they communicate their preferences directly. Clearly expressing one's thoughts and desires is of utmost importance, even if it may feel uncomfortable or awkward in the moment.

All of my kids played soccer during the fall season, while Andrew participated in both the spring and fall seasons. Having played soccer at the collegiate level myself, I can assess Andrew's skills and determine that he is not at the varsity level.

I made it a point to provide feedback to my kids after their games, including Andrew. I acknowledged that he played well on that particular day, but I also emphasized the importance of having a realistic understanding of where he stands compared to others at this point in his soccer journey. While I reassured him that there was nothing wrong with his performance, I wanted him to grasp the reality that pursuing a professional or highly competitive high school soccer career might not be feasible.

What frustrated me the most was the practice of the league providing participation trophies. These trophies often give the players a false sense of accomplishment and inflate their perception of their abilities. The truth is that many of them won't even make it to the next level as bench players, let alone achieve substantial success in the sport.

It's essential for young athletes to receive honest feedback and understand the level of dedication and talent required to excel in their chosen sport. While participation trophies may serve as a form of encouragement, they should not overshadow the importance of recognizing true achievements and motivating athletes to strive for improvement and excellence.

The same issue applies to the Advanced Gift Program. While all of my kids had to go through a rigorous testing process to get into the program, there were some kids who were able to join based solely on their parents' recommendations. It made me question the purpose and fairness of such a system.

Firstly, nobody would openly confront those who got in through backdoor methods, but it was widely known among everyone, including the kids themselves. It created a sense of unfairness and resentment, as those who truly earned their spot through testing had to witness others gaining admission through connections.

Secondly, it became evident that some of these kids who entered the program through favoritism or nepotism struggled to keep up once the advanced curriculum began. They faltered and fell behind, lacking the necessary skills and preparation that the testing process was designed to identify.

This situation not only highlighted the flaws in the selection process but also had a detrimental effect on the overall learning environment. It undermined the integrity of the program and hindered the progress of those who deserved to be there based on their abilities and hard work.

Upon graduating from high school, many students are shocked to find that more than half of their peers face difficulties that impact their self-esteem and overall functioning. The transition to the real world can be challenging, as they encounter new responsibilities and the absence of familiar support systems. Additionally, the competitive environment of middle/high school may have inflated their sense of self, making the adjustment even more difficult. Let's refrain from giving everyone a trophy and instead encourage them to earn what they truly deserve. While it may be tough or disappointing in the short term, this approach will ultimately lead to personal growth and improvement in the long run.

Chapter 27

Driving Lesson

Teaching driving lessons to Lauren feels like it was just yesterday. It's incredible to see how she has progressed over the past two years and is now prepared for her college journey.

I'm certain that Lauren's experience of learning to drive from me and her experience of teaching driving lessons are completely different.

I still remember the time when Lauren asked me what the name of the handlebar next to the passenger's seat was. Initially, I was thinking of it simply as the passenger handlebar. However, when Lauren informed me that it's commonly referred to as the "oh shit handle," I couldn't help but chuckle because it was indeed a humorous and accurate nickname for it.

Any parent will tell you that teaching your teenage kids how to drive can be an anxiety-inducing experience. The passenger side handlebar has certainly received its fair share of love and use over the years. I can definitely relate to that sentiment as well. During Lauren's first actual road test, there was a moment when she unintentionally drifted to the right due to a large truck approaching from the opposite side.

She expressed her fear by saying, "Daddy, that big truck was scary." In response, I reassured her, saying, "Trust the yellow line in between, stay in your lane. The truck won't come over here." It made me realize that in driving school, having an extra brake would provide them with a sense of control, but relying on the 'oh shit handle' and hoping for the best is the only safety measure we have as parents. Perhaps that's why statistics show that men tend to have shorter lifespans compared to their wives, as they often take on the role of navigating and protecting their loved ones on the road.

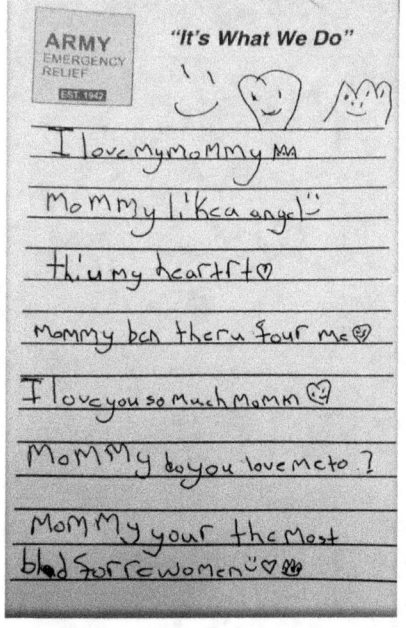

Here come my gray hairs, and maybe when Kristen starts driving, I'll lose even the few remaining ones I have left.

Do you know who extends their congratulations first, shortly after your kid obtains their driver's license? Surprisingly, it's the insurance company. As soon as your teen becomes a licensed driver, you'll receive a friendly reminder that their new status will likely lead to an increase in insurance premiums. It's a bittersweet moment, as you celebrate your child's milestone while also facing the reality of the financial implications that come with it. So, amidst the joy and pride, don't forget to brace yourself for that congratulatory message from the insurance company.

As parents, we can certainly say that we will never have a dull moment. From the exciting milestones and achievements to the unexpected challenges and surprises, parenting is an adventure filled with constant learning, growth, and moments that keep us on our toes. It's a journey that brings both joy and occasional chaos, making each day unique and memorable.

Chapter 28

6 Dollar Starbucks

When I married my wife Regina from Korea, I discovered many differences between us. Despite growing up in Korea during the same era, our memories of certain places were completely different. Seoul, the capital city, and a small southern town called Masan seemed like two different countries.

One notable distinction was the school cafeteria experience. When I attended middle school here, it was my first time encountering a cafeteria. However, in Regina's school in Seoul, cafeterias were readily available. My grade school friends often brought common packed lunches such as rice with fried kimchee, pink sausage, and fried eggs, and there were also some unique options like fried grasshoppers and fried pig intestine that could occasionally be seen. Unfortunately, a saddening aspect was that a few students couldn't afford to bring anything for lunch. They would often leave early during lunchtime to wait in the playground for others to finish their meals so they could play together. Although we were aware of this, including myself, we were too young to offer much help with what little we had. Regina had never witnessed anything quite like that in her school.

Regina definitely belonged to the middle class in Korea, although she used to perceive herself as poor compared to her friends. However, after many years of living together, Regina no longer disputes that statement with me. She has mentioned to me that her family goes out to eat in a restaurant at least once a week. Her dad often buys a couple of fried chickens to bring home, and there are always plenty of leftovers for all three girls.

In contrast to Regina's experience, my thrifty dad never took us out to eat. The only occasions we dined out were for weddings, funerals, and one of our graduations, usually when we had to travel to attend them. Even then, we would always choose the most budget-friendly options on the menu. However, despite the limited opportunities to eat out, my three sisters, brother, and I found immense happiness in those moments.

When Regina and I got married and moved into our first home, our financial situation was tight. We managed to furnish our living and dining room by spending less than 100 bucks on a couple of couches, a few chairs, and tables from a garage sale. I am truly grateful to Regina for standing by my side during those challenging times.

However, trouble began when we started to have a little more money, and Regina expressed her desire to dine out occasionally. Despite my father's frugal teachings, I often found myself at odds with Regina when it came to what I perceived as wasteful spending. However, as many married individuals can attest, it's challenging to win against your wife's wishes. Eventually, we started going out to eat more frequently, especially when Regina was pregnant. She would often crave various Korean foods that required us to drive for hours to find the perfect spot.

Being served by someone else truly brings a different experience. Sitting somewhere outside of our usual surroundings with our loved ones allows for a unique level of conversation and connection.

In the beginning, all I noticed on the menu was the price. I couldn't fully enjoy the time or the food. All I could think about was how much money I could save if I bought the ingredients and made the dish myself. I calculated that it would save us a significant amount of money, which we could then use for other purposes.

However, after a few months, I started to realize that there was more to dining out than just the cost. I began to appreciate the experience as a whole. It wasn't as bad as I initially thought. This was my first time truly understanding the joy of dining out, and I came to the realization that it wasn't all about the money.

Yes, dining out involves spending money, but in a way, it's similar to buying a luxury item for personal satisfaction. Just as purchasing a luxury item brings a sense of pleasure and indulgence, dining out offers a similar experience. It's about treating yourself and enjoying the ambience, service, and creativity that come with eating at a restaurant.

So, while I still consider the cost, I've learned to appreciate the value of the experience itself. Dining out is not just about the food; it's about the memories created, the connections made, and the overall enjoyment that comes with it.

I often wish my parents could have afforded to dine out occasionally. It could have positively impacted our family relationship and made it stronger today. Dining out creates shared experiences and allows for relaxation and deeper connections. It introduces new flavors and cultures, fostering conversation and broadening our horizons. It would have added a touch of celebration to our lives and created lasting memories.

Every time Regina expressed a desire to buy a 6-dollar latte from Starbucks, I found it difficult to understand the value of spending that much money. I would often question why we couldn't just opt for a dollar coffee from McDonald's instead. However, my perspective has shifted over time. I now realize that the cost of the latte wasn't the important factor; it was a way for me to show my love and support for my wife. It became a small gesture of pride for her, carrying that cup around the campus, and the 6 dollars spent became a meaningful investment in our relationship.

Interestingly, ever since my reaction changed towards her desire for the 6-dollar latte, Regina still occasionally indulges in it, but her craving for the drink has significantly decreased. It made me realize that just like how very wealthy individuals don't have to wear name brand clothing to showcase their wealth, the value of the drink itself became less important compared to the overall experience and connection we share.

Chapter 29

Everyone has Their Own Reasoning

Every time our family goes on a trip, it seems like we often pass by random cemeteries along the side of the highway. It's a somber reminder of the cycle of life and the inevitability of mortality.

I always remind my kids to offer prayers for the souls, especially those who may have been forgotten, including members of our own family. Besides, you should try doing that with your family, as when we pray for those souls, we often find ourselves avoiding traffic tickets.

Once, I asked my kids to imagine a scenario where God came back and offered those who were buried the chance to come back to life. I wondered what compelling stories each of the deceased would share, their reasons to return. Perhaps some would have heart-wrenching and valid reasons that even God could not deny. It's a thought-provoking concept that emphasizes the diverse experiences and stories that make up each person's life.

The fact that we are still alive while others have passed away can be seen as a matter of circumstance and fate. Some might argue that it's not fair, but ultimately, it is what it is.

I want my kids to recognize the value of their lives, even when things don't go their way or when they feel the system is unfair or they're not being treated reasonably. It's true that as humans, we have constructed systems that may struggle to encompass the intricacies and complexities of life. Nevertheless, it's crucial to acknowledge that our existing rules and regulations form the governing framework of our society. Though they have their limitations, these guidelines provide structure and serve as a basis for societal functioning. Furthermore, it's important to remember that your life is valuable and that your family cares about you.

Once, during my high school years, I experienced the tragic loss of a friend who took his own life. It deeply disturbed me and left a lasting impact. It is crucial to have open conversations with your kids about this sensitive topic from time to time.

When it comes to parenting, everyone has their own reasoning. Parenting styles, priorities, and choices can vary based on individual experiences, values, and circumstances. These differences in approach and decision-making reflect the diverse perspectives and beliefs of different individuals. Ultimately, this diversity in reasoning adds richness and depth to the collective experience of parenthood.

Chapter 30

Fair vs Urgent

Although my church teaches us to help the poor every day, I have noticed a recurring situation at busy street corners where individuals ask for money. In these instances, some believe that it is a test from God and that we should not turn a blind eye. However, I have chosen to teach my kids differently. I explain to them the potential outcomes of giving money in these situations, which often involve it being spent on drugs or alcohol. I have found that my observations align with reality, as when I ask these individuals how they plan to use the money right after giving it to them, they respond negatively, indicating that they have no intention of using it responsibly.

If someone is hungry, it can be beneficial to provide them with food. Buying them a meal or directing them to local resources like food banks or soup kitchens is a compassionate way to address their immediate need for sustenance.

When someone expresses a need for money, it can be more impactful to assist them in finding a job or connecting them with employment resources. By offering support in this manner, we can help individuals gain financial stability and independence.

If you find yourself in a situation where you don't have the time or resources to provide direct assistance, such as food or water, offering money might appear as a quick solution. However, it's crucial to recognize that there may be circumstances where you lack the means or ability to directly assist individuals in need. In such cases, it's understandable that refraining from immediate action may be a best practical approach.

My family experienced a time when we desperately needed jobs and assistance to establish ourselves and have a chance at success. We never relied on any handouts but instead worked tirelessly to improve our situation. In all my encounters with individuals in need, I have never seen a beggar sign explicitly asking for money, but rather pleading for help in finding any employment and transforming their lives for the better.

Living in a border city, I am constantly exposed to news stories about the influx of illegal immigrants. My church has taken a stance of providing aid and support to those in need, and I have contributed my share to support these efforts. However, while I understand that every migrant has a unique story and migration has been a part of human history for thousands of years, I cannot condone illegal behavior. It's important to recognize the complexities surrounding immigration and the individual circumstances that drive people to migrate. While it is crucial to provide humanitarian assistance to those in need, it is equally important to address immigration issues through legal channels and promote strict policies that ensure the safety and well-being of both migrants and the host communities.

We cannot ignore the importance of addressing urgent needs, but it is also crucial to consider the broader impact and long-term solutions. While it may be tempting to solely focus on immediate crises, such as the food crisis in Africa, overlooking fairness and sustainable solutions can perpetuate the cycle of need.

Addressing urgent needs without considering fairness and systemic change can lead to temporary relief but may not create lasting impact.

Likewise, when it comes to addressing student debt forgiveness and affirmative action in college admissions, a balanced approach is essential. While providing relief to students burdened by debt is important, it is vital to consider the long-term implications and fairness to all stakeholders involved.

Student debt forgiveness has the potential to alleviate the financial burden on individuals, enabling them to pursue opportunities and contribute to the economy. However, it is crucial to carefully assess the feasibility and potential consequences of such a policy. It is important to ensure that any measures taken do not undermine the value of education or create unintended negative impacts. Balancing the benefits of debt relief with the need for responsible financial decisions is important to maintain fairness and encourage responsible behavior.

Affirmative action in college admissions aims to promote diversity and equal opportunities. It can play a role in addressing historical inequalities. However, it is essential to continually evaluate its effectiveness and ensure that it does not lead to unfair advantages or discrimination against individuals who do not belong to the historically disadvantaged groups. Striking a balance between promoting diversity and fairness in college admissions is crucial to creating an inclusive and just society.

No one wants to see their children being penalized for following rules and regulations. It is important to discourage unfair behavior and ensure that rewards and opportunities are based on merit and adherence to established guidelines. Evaluating someone's worth should be based on their contributions and achievements, rather than solely on their immediate needs for survival. If someone requires more assistance to meet their needs, society should focus on helping them work harder or smarter, rather than simply providing handouts.

Urgent needs should never be used as a justification for mistreating individuals who have followed the rules. Instead, it is crucial to find ways to address urgent needs while maintaining fairness and upholding the integrity of established systems and regulations. It is important to strike a balance between addressing immediate crises and ensuring that everyone is treated fairly within the existing framework. By doing so, we can create a society that supports those in need without compromising the principles of fairness and merit.

The balance between addressing the immediate needs of individuals who require help and considering those who have followed the rules and regulations, patiently waiting their turn, is a complex dilemma. Society grapples with the challenge of striking a balance between compassion and fairness. While it is important to respond promptly to urgent situations and provide assistance to those in need, it is equally crucial to uphold the principles of fairness and equity for all individuals.

Chapter 31

Misunderstanding

About 6 years ago, my dad passed away in Korea, and receiving a late-night phone call from my sister, especially considering that my family rarely communicates outside of weekend daytime, was understandably concerning. Such deviations from my usual routines served as an indication that something important or unusual had occurred. During that time, it was Memorial Weekend, and the U.S. embassy was closed. Thankfully, my brother, who happened to be a special agent in a three-letter federal agency, contacted the embassy for off-hour support to assist my mom, who was with my dad and unsure of what to do.

After my dad's passing, my second older sister, my brother, and I quickly obtained plane tickets to travel to Korea for the funeral. The situation was challenging for my mom, who was in shock and unable to recall our phone numbers to contact us. Since my dad was a U.S. citizen who passed away overseas, we had to seek clearance from the embassy before proceeding with the burial or cremation. The embassy needed to ensure there were no suspicions of foul play or any other suspicious activities surrounding his death.

During this time, the hospital in Korea charged us on a daily basis for preserving my dad's body and wouldn't proceed without clearance from the U.S. embassy. Knowing that my dad wanted to be buried in the U.S. alongside his mom (my grandmother), we made the decision to have him cremated. However, we were shocked to discover that Korea charged foreigners a significantly higher rate for cremation compared to their own citizens – approximately 30 times more.

Since my dad passed away near Busan, my brother Louis had to make multiple trips to Seoul to complete the necessary paperwork. Thankfully, the process was relatively straightforward for us.

When my other sister reached out to someone in her Korean church in Ohio, she was informed that in similar situations, it took more than 10 months to obtain the clearance letter from the embassy. This information highlighted the potential variations in processing times and added an additional layer of complexity to the situation. Indeed, having Louis's special agent badge proved to be a significant advantage during this difficult time. It facilitated our communication with the embassy and sped up obtaining the necessary clearances. His badge provided credibility and helped navigate the bureaucratic procedures more efficiently.

During a moment of rest in our old house in Korea, Louis and I had a meaningful conversation. He had just received a new assignment from Pittsburgh to Virginia and was busy with the process of moving to a new apartment.

Unfortunately, during this hectic period, our sister called him with the news of our dad's passing.

To compound the challenges, Tracy, his wife, who was also eight months pregnant at the time, confronted him about cheating, suspecting that he had been involved with another girl for months. Tracy showed him a Facebook picture that her friend had sent, seemingly suggesting my brother's infidelity. However, it turned out that the person in the picture was our first cousin David, with whom we had lost contact since our first year in the States. Louis was genuinely taken aback by Tracy's accusation and had no idea what she was talking about.

Furthermore, Louis couldn't believe that Tracy didn't confront him right away, as it is common for Asian, Latino, or Black girls to address such issues promptly. The timing of her questioning during this already chaotic week added to the overwhelming nature of the situation.

It seems that there is a strong resemblance within my family, with my brother resembling my grandfather, my uncle resembling my grandfather as well, and I resembling my father more than Louis. Similarly, my cousin David bears a resemblance to his own father. Tracy, being Caucasian, may not have been familiar with the family resemblances or cultural cues that you are accustomed to, making it harder for her to distinguish the differences. It was also difficult for me to discern the distinctions initially.

Due to the strained relationship between my dad and uncle, they were not invited to Louis's wedding in Philadelphia. Consequently, Tracy was not aware of the existence of our first cousins who live in nearby states. The lack of knowledge about these cousins likely contributed to the confusion surrounding the Facebook picture and Tracy's misunderstanding.

Well, when Louis brought the ashes to the state, some-how my uncle and David found out about the funeral. Louis told me that both of them showed up at the burial site. After Tracy saw David with her own eyes, it became clear to her, and my brother didn't have to explain himself any further.

Chapter 32

Snake and Cow

My eldest sister, Juliana, faced a formidable journey to establish herself as a respected paralegal in the government's office. Achieving this status demanded her unwavering determination, tireless effort, and the ability to overcome numerous challenges along the way. In contrast, my other sisters pursued more conventional paths, with one becoming a high school teacher and the other a college professor.

Juliana's different path was not a voluntary choice but rather a result of external circumstances or being forced into it, a different path compared to the rest of us siblings. Instead of pursuing a professional career, she prioritized supporting the family and took on the responsibility of contributing to our well-being. This was especially crucial during our early stages of immigration when our dad couldn't provide much financial support. Both my mom and Juliana became hardworking "workhorses" to generate the much-needed income. Juliana's influence and dedication to supporting the family played a significant role in shaping the success of the rest of my siblings' professional careers.

Fortunately, my dad's diligent savings habits allowed us to rely on his savings for extended support during that time. As I grew older, I learned the importance of being financially independent, which involves saving, earning, and investing. While my dad excelled at the first step of saving, he wasn't able to progress to the next two steps of generating more income and investing. Nonetheless, his emphasis on saving provided a foundation for me to understand the value of financial independence and strive towards achieving it through a well-rounded approach.

Juliana had a friend named Mrs. Ghim who married early and had two young boys, just like another immigrant family navigating the trials of raising a family in a new country. Interestingly, the two boys, who were only a year apart, had contrasting reactions to Mrs. Ghim's special lunch of Korean-style California rolls made with spam and rice. The younger boy expressed joy and gratitude for having Kim-bob for lunch, while the older one had a different preference and requested a peanut butter and jelly sandwich instead.

When Mrs. Ghim wanted to know details, it appears that when the younger boy's friends found out about the Kim-bob lunch, they were excited and intrigued by the new food, which made the younger boy popular among his peers. On the other hand, the older boy had a less positive experience as his peer's made fun of the smell of Kim-bob and treated him poorly because of it. The younger one appears to have a more outgoing and assertive personality, as evidenced by his excitement over trying new foods and quickly becoming popular among his friends. In contrast, the older boy seems to have a more passive personality, as he faced mistreatment and was affected by the negative reactions of his peers towards the smell of the food.

Having three kids of my own has completely changed my perspective on the story. Experiencing parenthood and witnessing how my own children navigate social situations has given me a deeper understanding and empathy for the challenges they may encounter. The story that Mrs. Ghim shared about her boys' differing experiences with their lunch truly emphasizes the significant impact of social dynamics on children. It reminds me of the importance of fostering an environment where children feel accepted and respected for their individuality and cultural backgrounds. Indeed, just like how snakes and cows both drink dew from the morning grass and create different things with it, different children in the same scenario can react and have vastly different outcomes. While cows produce milk, a nourishing and essential resource for humans, snakes produce venom, a potentially harmful and dangerous substance.

When I reflect on my high school years, I recall a few opportunities to go on field trips to Six Flags. However, I chose not to seize those chances, as I was well aware of the impact it would have on our limited budget. I didn't even inform my family about the upcoming field trips, understanding the financial strain it would impose. Despite my disappointment, I did not feel anger. Instead, this experience taught me the significance of financial responsibility and served as motivation to improve my financial situation. I made a personal promise that, in the future, when I have children of my own, I will strive to provide them with better opportunities to enjoy such trips.

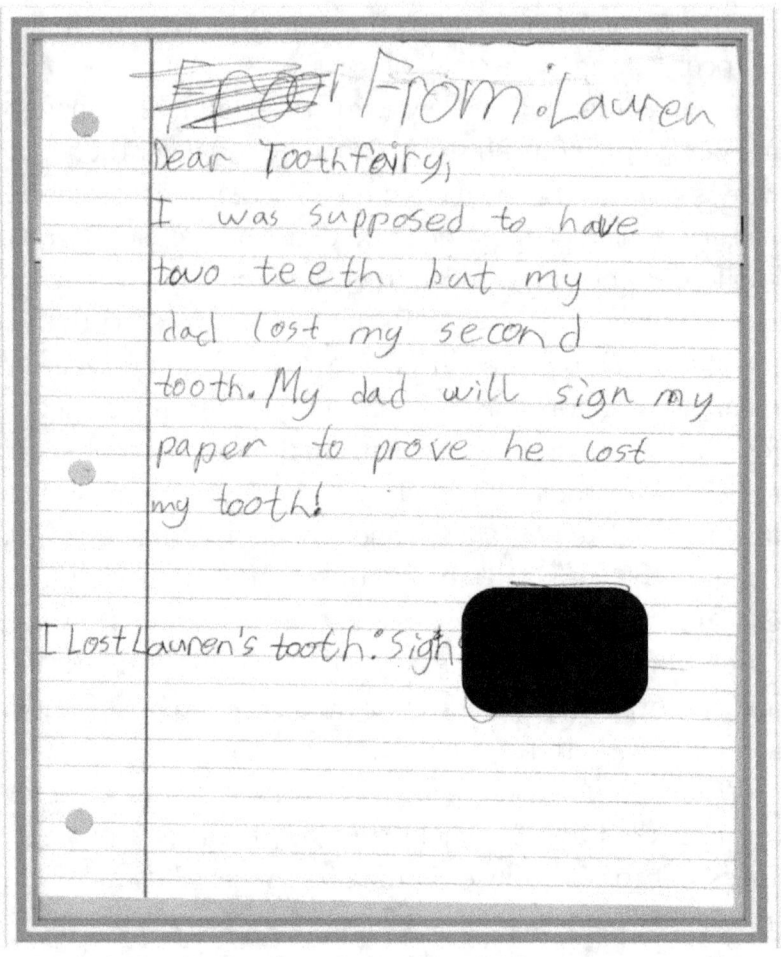

Dear Toothfairy,
I was supposed to have two teeth but my dad lost my second tooth. My dad will sign my paper to prove he lost my tooth!

I lost Lauren's tooth. Sign

Hearing those words from Andrew filled me with confidence, as it indicated that I have instilled the right values in my children thus far.

The Stories of Childhood

STRONG BEGINNINGS Observation C.

Child's Name: Lauren	Date: 3-2-11
Observer Name: Mrs. Perez	Room: SBA

Directions: Write an objective "snapshot" observation, then circle one goal and write 1+ objective numbers belo

Lauren joined her friends at the Tic-Tac-Toe table today. She sat down and waited for her friend to pass out game cards so she could play.

3B. VIA63 - Participate in the group life of their classroom.

GOAL: I. Approaches to Learning   II. Social/Emotional Development   OBJECTIVE(S): _____
III. Language and Literacy   IV. Mathematics   V. Science and Technology
VI. Social Studies   VII. The Arts   VIII. Physical Development

ACTIVITY PLANS BASED ON OBSERVATIONS: floor puzzle for group work VIA63

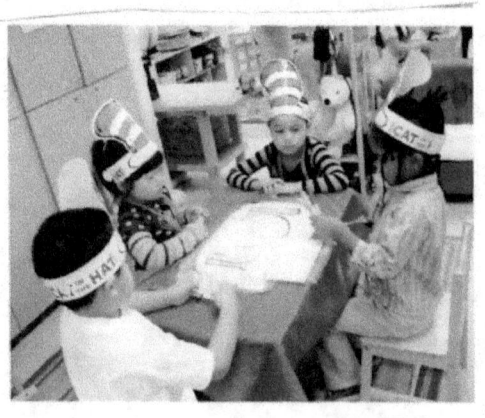

STRONG BEGINNINGS OBSERVATION CARD

Child's Name: Lauren   Date: 3-2-11
Observer Name: Mrs Perez   Room: SB A

Directions: Write an objective "snapshot" observation, then circle one goal and write 1+ objective numbers below.

Lauren followed her mom to the math station today to work on Dr. Suess math. She sat down with a friend and got a pencil and then began to work with each-other to solve 1x1 digit adding.

SB IVA34 - Count and know that the last number tells how many.

GOAL: I. Approaches to Learning II. Social/Emotional Development   OBJECTIVE(S): IV
III. Language and Literacy IV. Mathematics V. Science and Technology
VI. Social Studies VII. The Arts VIII. Physical Development

ACTIVITY PLANS BASED ON OBSERVATIONS: Use linking cubes to create patterns IVD 44-45

PRESCHOOL OBSERVATION CARD

Child's Name: _Lauren_   Date: _3-25-09_

Observer Name: _Mary_   Room: _DR 1 B_

Directions: Write an objective "snapshot" observation, then circle one goal and write 1+ objective numbers below.

Lauren moved the mouse around then itouched the screen and said "Teacher Mary, Hammer!" excidedly pointing to the pic of hammer.

GOAL: I. Self Others Behavior   II. Gross Motor Fine Motor   OBJECTIVE(S): _22-1_
III. Learn/Solve Logical Thinking Representation/Symbolic   IV. Listen/Speak Reading/Writing

ACTIVITY PLANS BASED ON OBSERVATIONS:

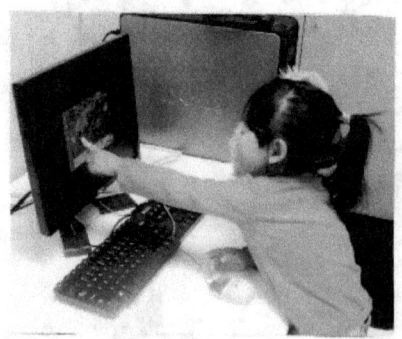

STRONG BEGINNINGS Observation C.

Child's Name: Lauren To   Date: 3-31-11

Observer Name: Mrs. Perez   Room: 2B-A

Directions: Write an objective "snapshot" observation, then circle one goal and write 1+ objective numbers belo

Today Lauren waited her turn
to practice throwing a soft
ball to make a basket. She stood
standing still with her feet flat.
She used eye coordination. She then
reached up and tip-toed - and threw
the ball high - and made a basket.

2B: VIIIA77 - Large movement skill using
upper body coordination to throw.

GOAL: I. Approaches to Learning II. Social/Emotional Development   OBJECTIVE(S): _VIII_
III. Language and Literacy   IV. Mathematics   V. Science and Technology
VI. Social Studies VII. The Arts VIII. Physical Development

ACTIVITY PLANS BASED ON OBSERVATIONS: Use basketball to
coordinate balance and stamina to Dribble.

VIIA77

Flat foot

Tip-toe Yeah! I made
it!

STRONG BEGINNINGS Observation Card

Child's Name: Lauren to

Date: April 24, 201

Observer Name: Mrs Perry

Room: 2B A

Directions: Write an objective "snapshot" observation, then circle one goal and write 1+ objective numbers below.

Lauren come to the Carpet and Sat on her chair. She put her feet on the floor and then hands in her lap. She Sat and waited for her friend to finish sharing, then it would be her turn next.

3B-1A2 Show initiative /self direction

GOAL: I Approaches to Learning II Social/Emotional Development OBJECTIVE(S): I
III. Language and Literacy IV. Mathematics V. Science and Technology
VI. Social Studies VII. The Arts VIII. Physical Development

ACTIVITY PLANS BASED ON OBSERVATIONS: respond to the
100- restaurant card

STRONG BEGINNINGS OBSERVATION C.

Child's Name: Lauren TO
Date: 4-13-11
Observer Name: mrs pison
Room: SB-A

Directions: Write an objective "snapshot" observation, then circle one goal and write 1+ objective numbers below

Lauren was working with
her friends to tear up paper
and add water to observe
and make an inquiry of what
will happen. Lauren helped
her friends cut paper and, said,
"It's soaking up?

SB-VA47 - use scientific inquiry -
collect into her observing.

GOAL: I. Approaches to Learning II. Social/Emotional Development OBJECTIVE(S): V
III. Language and Literacy IV. Mathematics V. Science and Technology
VI. Social Studies VII. The Arts VIII. Physical Development

ACTIVITY PLANS BASED ON OBSERVATIONS: Smell aroma from
popcorn guess what it is. Y um.

PRESCHOOL OBSERVATION CARD

Child's Name: Lauren   Date: 1-2-09
Observer Name: Mary   Room: DR

Directions: Write an objective "snapshot" observation, then circle one goal and write 1+ objective numbers below.

While doing art making a flag,
CG asked Lauren to put glue on the
star and put it on the blue part of the flag.
Lauren picked up glue and squeezed
it on the blue. CG then said you need
to put glue on the star and Lauren
picked up her star and looked at
CG.

GOAL: I. **Self** Others Behavior   II. Gross Motor Fine Motor   OBJECTIVE(S): 40-1
II. **Learn/Solve** Logical Thinking Representation/Symbolic   IV. **Listen/Speak** Reading/Writing

ACTIVITY PLANS BASED ON OBSERVATIONS:

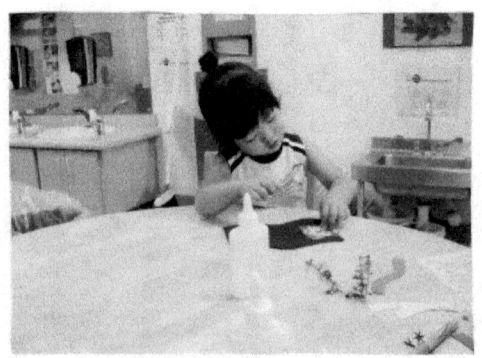

PRESCHOOL OBSERVATION CARD

Child's Name: _Lauren_   Date: _7/1/09_
Observer Name: _Mary_   Room: _DP_

Directions: Write an objective "snapshot" observation, then circle one goal and write 1+ objective numbers below.

Lauren used the glue bottle +
squeezed glue on the sand, she then
picked up a small shell and placed
it on the glue.

GOAL: I. Self Others Behavior   II. Gross Motor (Fine Motor)   OBJECTIVE(S): _E 20 1_
III. Learn/Solve Logical Thinking   Representation/Symbolic   IV. Listen/Speak Reading/Writing

ACTIVITY PLANS BASED ON OBSERVATIONS: _will work on more_
fine motor skills with
holding a crayon and drawing

INFANT-TODDLER OBSERVATION CARD

Child's Name: Andrew   Date: Aug 2010

Observer Name: Tonya   Room: M. Moments

Directions: Write an objective "snapshot" observation, then circle one goal and write 1+ objective numbers below.

Andrew used his (R) hand to hold the marker as he drew all over the paper. He was able to make some circular movements w/ the marker. He then used a spray bottle to spray his paper to make his rainbow art.

GOAL: 1. Themselves 2. Moving 3. World 4. Communicating   OBJECTIVE(S): 2.9

ACTIVITY PLANS BASED ON OBSERVATIONS: Making shapes w/pencils

INFANT-TODDLER OBSERVATION CARD

Child's Name: Andrew   Date: Sept 2010
Observer Name: Tonya   Room: M. Moments

Directions: Write an objective "snapshot" observation, then circle one goal and write 1+ objective numbers below.

As Andrew sat in the swing he
began calling "Tonya" over and over.
When Teacher Tonya said "Yes Andrew"
he said "Help, please!"

GOAL: 1. Themselves 2. Moving 3. World 4. Communicating   OBJECTIVE(S): _____

ACTIVITY PLANS BASED ON OBSERVATIONS:

INFANT-TODDLER OBSERVATION CARD

Child's Name: _Andrew 10_   Date: _April 2011_
Observer Name: _Tonya Wall_   Room: _M. Moments_

Directions: Write an objective "snapshot" observation, then circle one goal and write 1+ objective numbers below.

Andrew waited for teachers to raise the parachute he then ran under it, laughing the whole time. When he came out the other side he ask "I do it again?"

GOAL: 1. Themselves 2. Moving 3. World ④. Communicating   OBJECTIVE(S): _4._

ACTIVITY PLANS BASED ON OBSERVATIONS:

INFANT -TODDLER OBSERVATION CARD

Child's Name: *Andrew To*   Date: *7-09*
Observer Name: *Jo Dean*   Room: *Little Wonders* -A
Directions: Write an objective "snapshot" observation, then circle one goal and write 1+ objective numbers below.

Andrew sitting on mat, holding
teething ring, chewing on it.
(Teething time)

GOAL: 1. Themselves 2. Moving 3. World 4. Communicating   OBJECTIVE(S): *11*

ACTIVITY PLANS BASED ON OBSERVATIONS:
See if he can put toy into container

INFANT -TODDLER OBSERVATION CARD

Child's Name: *Andrew T.*   Date: *Sept 2008*
Observer Name: *Jo Doan*   Room: *Little Wonders*

Directions: Write an objective "snapshot" observation, then circle one goal and write 1+ objective numbers below.

Andrew laying on his back in
donut cushion, holding onto a scarf
squeezing it, looking at or talking
to him.

GOAL: 1. Themselves 2. Moving (3. World) 4. Communicating   OBJECTIVE(S): *11*

ACTIVITY PLANS BASED ON OBSERVATIONS:

Next time I'll give him a toy.
That squeaks when he squeezes it.

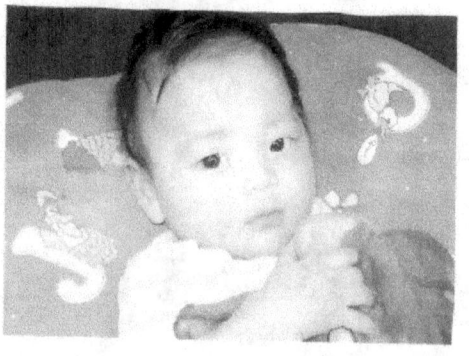

INFANT-TODDLER OBSERVATION CARD

Child's Name: Andrew Date: July 2010
Observer Name: Tonya Room: Magic Moments

Directions: Write an objective "snapshot" observation, then circle one goal and write 1+ objective numbers below.

As Andrew began pushing the shopping
cart through the sand it became stuck.
He then turned and looked behind himself as he began walking backwards, while
still holding the cart, until he was out of
the sand.

GOAL: 1. Themselves 2. Moving 3. World 4. Communicating OBJECTIVE(S): 3 & 4

ACTIVITY PLANS BASED ON OBSERVATIONS: Pretend play - in kitchen area

INFANT-TODDLER OBSERVATION CARD

Child's Name: Andrew To   Date: 6-09
Observer Name: Brandy   Room: Little Wonders

Directions: Write an objective "snapshot" observation, then circle one goal and write 1+ objective numbers below.

Andrew is clapping with is friends while CG sings
clapping song.

GOAL: 1. Themselves 2. Moving 3. World 4. Communicating   OBJECTIVE(S):

ACTIVITY PLANS BASED ON OBSERVATIONS:

Encourage him to say "yay" while clapping

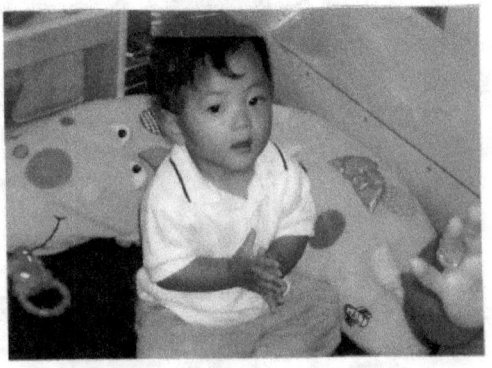

INFANT-TODDLER OBSERVATION CARD

Child's Name: _Andrew TO_   Date: _Oct 2008_
Observer Name: _Jo Doan_   Room: _Little Wonders_

Directions: Write an objective 'snapshot' observation, then circle one goal and write 1+ objective numbers below.

Andrew smiling at another baby
and reaching toward her face
while laying on mat

GOAL: 1. Themselves 2. Moving 3. World (4. Communicating)   OBJECTIVE(S): _18_

ACTIVITY PLANS BASED ON OBSERVATIONS:

Show Andrew pictures of familiar
objects to get his reaction to the pictures.

General Documentation for A   , E   , Kristen To
May 16, 2017

Kristen and A   were at the light table when E   dragged a chair over to play with them. A   used the square magnetic blocks to build her creation. Kristen was trying to make a box out of the square magnetic blocks aslo. E   grabbed some blocks and said " I'm gonna make a house for my mommy."

Associated Dimensions & Levels | May 16, 2017

✓ 2c. Interacts with peers

✓ 3a. Balances needs and rights of self and others

✓ 7a. Uses fingers and hands

✓ 9b. Speaks clearly

✓ 11e. Shows flexibility and inventiveness in thinking

General Documentation for Kristen To

May 3, 2017

Kristen used her hands and feet to climb up the pole on the adventurescape at Volunteer Park. When she reached the top, she walked over to the slide and slid down. Kriisten decided to climb up the pole again.

Associated Dimensions & Levels | May 3, 2017

☑ 1b. Follows limits and expectations
 Preliminary Rating: Level 5

☑ 1c. Takes care of own needs appropriately
 Preliminary Rating: Level 6

☑ 5. Demonstrates balancing skills
 Preliminary Rating: Level 6

☑ 7a. Uses fingers and hands
 Preliminary Rating: Level 5

General Documentation for Kristen To
April 25, 2017

Kristen went into the reading center and took out the Tucker the turtle set. Kristen set the turtle by her and opened up the story book. Kristen turned the pages one at a time and looked at the pictures in the story book. Kristen cleaned her messes up when she was done.

Associated Dimensions & Levels | April 25, 2017

☑ 1b. Follows limits and expectations ⊜
   Preliminary Rating: Level 5

▩ 1c. Takes care of own needs appropriately ⊜

☑ 7a. Uses fingers and hands ⊜
   Preliminary Rating: Level 6

☑ 17a. Uses and appreciates books ⊜
   Preliminary Rating: Level 4

General Documentation for A_____, Kristen To

July 14, 2017

A____ and Kristen both asked if they could go into housekeeping. A____ took the baby doll out and went to sit on the couch. Kristen got the baby doll blanket out and covered her lap as she went to sit on the couch. They both were laughing . I asked them what they were playing. Kristen replied " We are doing a picnic."

Associated Dimensions & Levels | July 14, 2017

☑ 1c. Takes care of own needs appropriately ⊕

☑ 2d. Makes friends ⊕

☑ 7a. Uses fingers and hands ⊕

☑ 9b. Speaks clearly ⊕

☑ 11e. Shows flexibility and inventiveness in thinking ⊕

☑ 14b. Engages in sociodramatic play ⊕

General Documentation for Kristen To

July 5, 2017

Kristen sat at the art table with another friend.   Kristen was looking in the container full of beads and picked out a bead.   Kristen strung it on the plastic string that she was holding.   Kristen continued to string beads until she said " I'm done now."   Kristen then asked " Can you tie it for me?"   I tied the string for her and she put her necklace on to show her friends.

Associated Dimensions & Levels | July 5, 2017

- ☑ 1c. Takes care of own needs appropriately
  Preliminary Rating: Level 6

- ☑ 2c. Interacts with peers
  Preliminary Rating: Level 3

- ☑ 7a. Uses fingers and hands
  Preliminary Rating: Level 6

- ☑ 9b. Speaks clearly
  Preliminary Rating: Level 5

- ☑ 9c. Uses conventional grammar
  Preliminary Rating: Level 4

- ☑ 11e. Shows flexibility and inventiveness in thinking
  Preliminary Rating: Level 4

General Documentation for B   , Kristen To
June 27, 2017

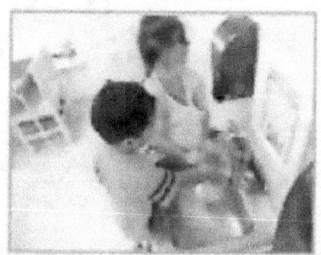

Kristen and Be   asked if the could go to the water table.   I asked them if they would like to help
me fill the water table. They both said yes. Kristen made sure the plastic jug was right under the
faucet as the water slowy started to fill up the jug. When the jug was full, B   helped Kristen to
carry it to the water table and they both helped to dump the water out of the it.

Associated Dimensions & Levels | June 27, 2017

☑ 1b. Follows limits and expectations

☑ 2a. Forms relationships with adults

☑ 2d. Makes friends

☑ 7a. Uses fingers and hands

☑ 8a. Comprehends language

☑ 8b. Follows directions

General Documentation for A⬛⬛⬛⬛⬛⬛, Kristen To
June 14, 2017

Kristen and A⬛⬛⬛ were sitting at the table together playing with the magnet set. A⬛⬛ took out a duck shaped magnet and put it on the magnetic board. Kristen reached into the jar and pulled out a star magnet and placed it next to the other start magnets on the board.

Associated Dimensions & Levels | June 14, 2017

☑ 1b. Follows limits and expectations ⚙

☑ 2d. Makes friends ⚙

☑ 7a. Uses fingers and hands ⚙

☑ 11a. Attends and engages ⚙

General Documentation for Kristen To
September 20, 2016

Kristen played the coloring game on the Ipad, after she finished she used her finger to erase what she had colored. She then started over and colored a new picture.

Associated Dimensions & Levels | September 20, 2016

☑ 7a. Uses fingers and hands ⓘ

☑ 11a. Attends and engages ⓘ

☑ 11d. Shows curiosity and motivation ⓘ

General Documentation for Kristen To

September 7, 2016

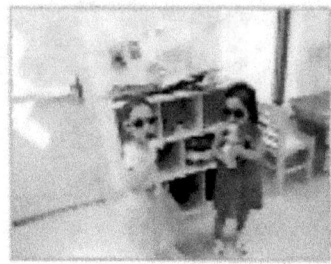

Kristen went to the music center with a friend.   She used the play microphone to start singing " Let it go."
Kristen walked around the table and sang along with twirling around .   When Kristen was done singing, she put
away her mircrophone and sunglasses and went to play in another center.

Associated Dimensions & Levels | September 7, 2016

☑ 1b. Follows limits and expectations ⓘ
  Preliminary Rating: Level 4

☑ 1c. Takes care of own needs appropriately ⓘ
  Preliminary Rating: Level 5

☑ 7a. Uses fingers and hands ⓘ
  Preliminary Rating: Level 5

☑ 34. Explores musical concepts and expression ⓘ
  Preliminary Rating: Level 1

☑ 35. Explores dance and movement concepts ⓘ
  Preliminary Rating: Level 1

General Documentation for Kristen To

Kristen asked"can S;   and me go in blocks" they went to the block center and picked up round blocks and pretended to put on makeup.

Associated Dimensions & Levels | August 30, 2016

☑ 1a. Manages feelings ⓘ

☑ 1b. Follows limits and expectations ⓘ

☑ 2c. Interacts with peers ⓘ

☑ 2d. Makes friends ⓘ

☑ 7a. Uses fingers and hands ⓘ

☑ 8a. Comprehends language ⓘ

☑ 10a. Engages in conversations ⓘ

☑ 11a. Attends and engages ⓘ

☑ 14a. Thinks symbolically ⓘ

☑ 14b. Engages in sociodramatic play ⓘ

About the Author

Youngchan Andrew To holds a Bachelor of Science degree in Mathematics from Penn State University. Commissioned through the Penn State Army ROTC program in 1999, he embarked on a career that intertwined his mathematical expertise with his military service. Following his initial academic pursuits, he pursued a Master of Science in Mathematics from New Mexico State University. This advanced degree further honed his mathematical acumen, equipping him with the skills necessary to excel in his future roles.

Currently serving as a dedicated mathematician at White Sands Missile Range (WSMR), Youngchan has established himself as a valuable asset within this critical institution. His contributions are informed not only by his educational background but also by his over two decades of experience in the field. Beyond his professional achievements, Youngchan's personal life is marked by his role as a proud father to three children. With a commitment to both family and work, he has demonstrated a capacity for balance and dedication. His enduring marriage of over 20 years to his partner, Regina, speaks to his ability to cultivate lasting relationships and maintain stability in all aspects of life.